Famous Stories
for Performance

HOLT, RINEHART AND WINSTON

A Harcourt Classroom Education Company

Austin • New York • Orlando • Atlanta • San Francisco
Boston • Dallas • Toronto • London

Requests for permission to make copies of any part of the work should be mailed to the following address: Permissions Department, Holt, Rinehart and Winston, 1120 South Capital of Texas Highway, Austin, Texas 78746-6487.

For permission to reprint copyrighted material, grateful acknowledgment is made to the following sources:

Columbia TriStar Television: Slightly adapted from *Brian's Song* by William Blinn. Copyright © 1971 by Screen Gems, a division of Columbia Pictures.

Rosemont Productions, Ltd.: *The Secret Garden,* written for television by Blanche Hanalis; based on the novel by Frances Hodgson Burnett. Copyright © 1987 by Rosemont Productions, Ltd.

Cover: (background, Times Square) © FPG International; (foreground, *Cats* company) © Nigel Teare.

The front cover shows a performance of the long-running musical *Cats,* a play based on T.S. Eliot's book of poems called *Old Possum's Book of Practical Cats.*

Printed in the United States of America

ISBN 0-03-055102-1

3 4 5 6 043 04 03 02

Contents

iii

The Secret Garden

Frances Hodgson Burnett
dramatized by Blanche Hanalis

Characters

(in order of appearance)

BEN WEATHERSTAFF: *the gardener at Misselthwaite Manor in England.*

MARY LENNOX: *an orphaned English girl who is sent from India to live at Misselthwaite Manor.*

CAPTAIN LENNOX, MRS. LENNOX: *Mary's parents.*

MRS. CRAWFORD: *a friend of the Lennoxes in India.*

COLONEL MCGRAW, LIEUTENANT BARNEY: *British officers serving in India.*

MRS. MEDLOCK: *housekeeper for Archibald Craven.*

JOHN: *footman for Archibald Craven.*

PITCHER: *servant for Archibald Craven.*

DICKON SOWERBY: *a boy of about twelve. His family is large and poor and lives in a cottage near Misselthwaite Manor.*

MARTHA SOWERBY: *a servant for Archibald Craven; Dickon's sister.*

BETTY: *scullery maid at Misselthwaite Manor.*

ARCHIBALD CRAVEN: *master of Misselthwaite Manor; a bitter widower who is also an invalid.*

COLIN CRAVEN: *Archibald's only child, about twelve years old.*

DR. CRAVEN: *Colin's doctor; Archibald's cousin.*

MRS. GORDY: *cook at Misselthwaite Manor.*

MRS. SOWERBY: *Martha and Dickon's mother.*

NURSE BOGGS: *Colin's nurse.*

LILIAS: *Archibald Craven's wife; Colin's mother.*

1

The *Secret Garden* is a **teleplay**—a play written for, and shown on, television. Since the play is designed for TV instead of the stage, the script includes many camera directions. These directions tell where a scene is set, how the characters read their lines, and how they should act. Camera directions also tell how close or far away the camera is and how it moves. As a reader, you can use these directions to imagine what you'd see if you were watching this play on TV.

Study the teleplay terms in the list below, and refer to it if you get confused. A teleplay or a **screenplay** (a script written for the movies) will contain these camera directions:

Fade In: the picture gradually appears on the screen.

Fade Out: the picture gradually disappears.

Cut to: a sudden change is made from one scene or character to another.

Dissolve to: a new scene is blended in with a scene being faded out.

Tight shot: a close-up camera shot.

Ext.: exterior (outdoors).

Int.: interior (indoors).

Long shot: a camera shot from far off.

Pan: a swiveling movement of the camera, from one side to the other.

Montage: Several images appear on the screen in quick succession.

Beat: pause.

Day: daytime scene.

Night: nighttime scene.

Scene number: scenes are numbered when the script goes into production to provide clear landmarks for revisions.

Act One

Fade In:

Opening titles appear over a succession of exterior shots.

1. **Ext.—Yorkshire moor—day**
   Wide on a moor with a stone gazebo off in the distance.

2. **Ext. roadway—day**
   An open touring car moves swiftly up the roadway toward the camera.

3. **Ext. signpost—day**
   The signpost reads MISSELTHWAITE MANOR. *The touring car drives past and we see that the car bears a large Red Cross on the door.*

4. **Ext. roadway—day**
   The car continues on its way, crossing a stone bridge.

5. **Ext. Misselthwaite Manor—day**
   A large imposing mansion that has seen better days. A tight shot of the centuries-old house reveals boarded windows and a building that is much in need of repair. The camera pans, and comes to a stop on BEN WEATHERSTAFF, *who is holding a black cat in his arms. About eighty,* BEN *has rheumy eyes and shaggy brows that give him an almost sinister appearance. Watching the approaching car, he seems angered by the intrusion.*

6. **Ext. roadway—day**
   The car continues on its way, passing the stone gazebo, which is also in a state of disrepair. BEN *peeks out around the corner of the house, staring at the approaching car.*

7. *Ext. touring car—day*
Camera is tight on the driver of the car, MARY LENNOX, a beautiful young woman in her early twenties. The car comes to a stop outside the manor.

8. *Ext. Misselthwaite Manor—day*
As she exits the car, we see that MARY is wearing the uniform of a British Red Cross transport driver. BEN continues to watch MARY as she walks. Suddenly, the black cat he has been holding leaps from BEN's arms and streaks away.

9. *Ext. vegetable garden—day*
As MARY passes through shot, the camera cuts to the cat moving along a wall—seemingly stalking MARY. MARY continues walking and there is suddenly heard the faint sound, filtered through time, of a little girl giggling. Again, the camera cuts to the cat as it continues to stalk MARY. MARY continues walking and there is suddenly the sound, from the past, of a little girl's voice.

LITTLE GIRL'S VOICE: "I never had any friends. When will it be spring? . . . We'll be driven out, like from the Garden of Eden."

10. *Ext. secret garden path—day*
MARY moves to a brick wall, pushes the ivy aside, and pulls a loose brick out of the wall. Whatever she expected to find inside the niche isn't there. Disappointed, she replaces the brick, moves to a tree, and leans against it. Lost in reverie, remembering another time, she touches the heart-shaped locket at her throat. Once again, there is the sound of a young girl speaking.

LITTLE GIRL'S VOICE: "I shall wear it always."

[Camera cuts to the cat, now in the tree just above MARY, poised to leap. As the cat leaps, we hear a scream.]

Cut to:

11. Int. bedroom—(Delhi, India, 1906)—on Mary—night
MARY, *ten years old, bolts upright in her bed, awakened by a scream. She's a thin, fair-haired, rather "plain" little girl whose arrogance and imperious manner do little to enhance her appearance.* MARY *calls her ayah.*

MARY: Saide?

[*There's no response.*]

MARY (*continuing*): Saide? (*Angry now*) You're supposed to come when I call you!

[*Frustrated and angry,* MARY *pushes the netting of her bed aside and gets up from the bed. In the distance there is the sound of adult laughter. She slowly crosses the room and we see a collection of children's dolls. Clutching her robe, she starts for the door, then looks back at a photograph on the bureau. The photo is a picture of* MARY's *parents,* CAPTAIN *and* MRS. LENNOX. MRS. LENNOX *is a luscious, dark-haired beauty.* CAPTAIN LENNOX, *a dashing young man in British Army dress uniform, is dark haired with a waxed dark moustache.*]

12. Int. hallway—night

MARY *walks slowly down the hall as the laughter of the adults grows louder. She peeks through the slats of a door leading into a dining room area. Through the slats, the camera reveals a group of eight adults seated at a formal dinner setting. All the women wear lovely gowns and the men are in British Army dress uniforms.*

13. Int. dining room—night

MRS. LENNOX *sits at one end of the table,* CAPTAIN LENNOX *at the other.* MRS. LENNOX, *as superficial as she is beautiful, ignores her other guests as she flirts with the handsome young officer to her right.* CAPTAIN LENNOX *is either oblivious or indifferent. His face is damp with perspiration and he looks ill. He suddenly looks up to see his wife's flirtation. Camera cuts back to show* MARY *looking through the slats of the door.* CAPTAIN LENNOX *reaches for his glass of wine and can barely raise it. He is obviously very sick. Camera on* MARY. *Angry at her mother for humiliating her father,* MARY *leaves the door and returns to her room.*

14. Int. Mary's bedroom—night
As MARY *enters and moves to the bed, she vents her anger at her mother on her absent nurse.*

MARY: I'll fix Saide in the morning! I'll put a snake in her millet!

[MARY *sits in a chair with one of her dolls in her lap. She speaks to the doll.*]

MARY: I'm going to read this lovely story about a Rajah and a tiger.

Cut to:

15. Int. dining room—night
MRS. LENNOX *is speaking animatedly.*

MRS. LENNOX: I just had the most marvelous idea! After the Governor's Ball, why don't we go for a breakfast picnic along the river?

[MRS. CRAWFORD, *one of the dinner guests, speaks out.*]

MRS. CRAWFORD: I doubt I'll feel much like a picnic after dancing all night.
MRS. LENNOX: Nonsense.
MRS. CRAWFORD: Besides, I shan't be going to the ball.

Steven's booked passage for me to England. He says there's some kind of plague in the provinces.

MRS. LENNOX (*gaily*): Oh, there's always some kind of plague in the provinces, Mrs. Crawford. I wouldn't let that stop me from going to the ball.

[MRS. LENNOX *lifts the small bell next to her plate. Rings it.* CAPTAIN LENNOX *wipes perspiration from his brow.* CAPTAIN LENNOX *rises. He stares blindly at his wife, then pitches face down on the table. Everyone with the exception of* MRS. LENNOX *races to be of help.*]

Cut to:

16. *Ext.* **blazing sky—sunset**
    A horn is being blown against the blood-red setting sun.

17. *Ext.* **street outside compound wall—day**
    Natives are fleeing the city, some on foot, others in carts pulled by bulls. Dust stirred up by the exodus casts a yellow haze. The sound is that of the bulls, the creaking carts, and the whips of the drivers. The frightened natives have only one thought: to escape the cholera that kills.

18. *Int.* **Mary's bedroom—day**
    MARY *awakens and calls out for her nurse.*

MARY: Saide . . . Saide!

[*There is no response and* MARY *moves to the window. From her point of view we again see the hundreds of natives fleeing the city.*]

Cut to:

19. *Int.* **servants' quarters—day**
    MARY's *nurse lies dead on the bed.* MARY *is curious but not frightened. She's seen death before. Beggars often die in the streets of Delhi.*

20. *Int. parents' room—day*

MARY's *father is lying comatose on the bed. Her mother, lying at the foot of the bed, is also feeling the final deadly effects of cholera.* MARY *enters the room.*

MARY: Mama, Saide is dead and there's no one to dress me or give me breakfast.

[MRS. LENNOX *groans.*]

21. *Int. dining room—day*

The remains of the interrupted dinner party are scattered on the table. Flies buzz around the platters of food. Some of the wineglasses are full, others have spilled and stained the damask cloth. There's evidence of hasty departure: a woman's wrap, a fan, an overturned chair.

MARY *comes into shot. She helps herself to food off the plates and drinks a glass of wine. Still thirsty, she drinks another.*

22. *Int. Mary's bedroom——day*

MARY *enters. The wine has gone to her head. She can barely walk and looks as if she is about to be sick. She stumbles toward the bed.*

MARY: I'm sick.

[*She plops herself down on the bed and goes to sleep.*]

23. *Ext. bungalow compound—day*

Natives are busily burning furniture, which people believed had been contaminated by the cholera. COL. MCGRAW *and* LIEUT. BARNEY *enter the compound.*

LIEUT. BARNEY: The servants may have taken the child with them. (*Suddenly spotting* MARY *standing in the doorway of her home*) She's here, Colonel . . . she's alive!

MARY (*annoyed*): Of course I'm alive, but Saide is dead, so I shall need a new ayah.

COL. MCGRAW (*distressed*): Poor child . . .

MARY (*haughty*): I am not a poor child. I am Mary Lennox and my father has a very important position at Government House.

LIEUT. BARNEY (*shaken*): She doesn't know, Colonel.

[COL. MCGRAW *hesitates, trying to find a way to soften the blow.*]

COL. MCGRAW (*compassionate*): I'm afraid there's no easy way to tell you this, child. I'm very sorry, my dear, but your parents are dead.

[*In the turmoil surrounding the three of them,* MARY *accidentally drops her favorite doll. She tries to go back for it, but a native scoops it up and the doll is thrown into the fire.*]

MARY (*screaming*): My doll . . . no, stop . . . give me my doll!

LIEUT. BARNEY: She doesn't understand, Colonel.

COL. MCGRAW: Well, it's hardly surprising. Look, we'll take you to Mrs. Crawford. She can look after you until other arrangements can be made.

MARY (*screaming*): Give me my doll, my doll!

[MARY *looks back in tears as her doll begins to burn. Riding off on horseback with* COL. MCGRAW, *she continues to stare back at the burning doll.*]

Cut to:

24. *Int. hotel dining room—dusk*

MARY *and* MRS. CRAWFORD *are seated at a table.* MARY *is ignoring her food as she stares ahead, stone faced. She wears mourning, a black jumper and black shoes and stockings. Her thin black coat is across the back of her chair*

and her black bonnet hangs from a spindle by its ribbons.
MRS. CRAWFORD *is in a smart traveling suit and hat and has a small fur around her shoulders.*

MRS. CRAWFORD (*kind*): Mary, you haven't touched your tea. Aren't you hungry?
MARY (*curt*): No.

[*A woman in her late sixties, tall and spare, enters the room and speaks to the headwaiter. She is* MRS. MEDLOCK, *and at first glance she's a somewhat formidable-looking woman. She approaches the table where* MRS. CRAWFORD *and* MARY *are seated.*]

MRS. MEDLOCK: Mrs. Crawford?
MRS. CRAWFORD (*warmly*): You must be Mrs. Medlock. Please, do sit down.

[*As* MRS. MEDLOCK *seats herself, she glances at* MARY, *curious about her.*]

MRS. CRAWFORD (*continuing*): Mary, this is Mrs. Medlock, who is going to take you to Yorkshire tomorrow.

[MARY *ignores the introduction.* MRS. MEDLOCK *manages to hide her annoyance at* MARY's *rudeness, but only barely.*]

MRS. MEDLOCK (*to* MRS. CRAWFORD): Mr. Craven said to thank you for bringing the little girl, ma'am.
MRS. CRAWFORD: It would have been unkind not to, since I was returning to England anyway.

[MARY *looks at* MRS. CRAWFORD *with contempt.*]

MRS. CRAWFORD (*continuing*): Will you have some tea?
MRS. MEDLOCK: No, thank you.
MRS. CRAWFORD: What time will you be calling for Mary tomorrow?
MRS. MEDLOCK: The train leaves at seven, so I'll be here at six.

MRS. CRAWFORD: So early?! Mary, will you be good enough to ask the desk clerk to send a porter up for your trunk a little before six?

[*Rising,* MARY *stares directly at* MRS. MEDLOCK *without saying a word. She then moves from the table.*]

MRS. CRAWFORD: She's a difficult child, Mrs. Medlock. But to be fair, it's not entirely her fault. If her mother had carried her pretty face into the nursery more often, Mary might not be quite so recalcitrant.

MRS. MEDLOCK: Neglected her, did she?

MRS. CRAWFORD: I know one shouldn't speak ill of the dead, but Mrs. Lennox was a very silly and shallow woman. She was embarrassed that Mary was plain, at least in her eyes, and Mary knew it.

MRS. MEDLOCK: Pity.

MRS. CRAWFORD: Yes. (*Warmly*) It's kind of Mr. Craven to take Mary, especially since they're not related.

MRS. MEDLOCK: There are no living relatives, but since Mr. Craven's and Captain Lennox's fathers were dear friends till they both passed on, young Mr. Craven felt obliged to give the little girl a home.

Cut to:

25. *Ext. English countryside—long shot—train—day*
    Though it's March and the fields are still fallow, the gently rolling landscape is lovely.

MRS. MEDLOCK'S VOICE: I've got some nice watercress sandwiches. Would you like one?

MARY'S VOICE (*curt*): I don't like English food, only Indian.

MRS. MEDLOCK'S VOICE: Well, English food is all you'll be getting at Misselthwaite Manor, so you'd better get used to it.

Cut to:

26. *Ext. roadway—dusk*

Carriage carrying MARY *and* MRS. MEDLOCK *to Misselthwaite Manor.*

MRS. MEDLOCK'S VOICE: Oh, it was different when Mrs. Craven was alive. She had cook make all sorts of foreign dishes. They took the recipes out of a book.

27. *Int. carriage—dusk*

MRS. MEDLOCK (*continuing*): Mr. Archibald—Mr. Craven, that is—didn't mind. She was such a sweet pretty thing. Nobody thought she'd marry him, not with that hump on his back, but she did.

[MARY*'s intrigued in spite of herself.*]

MARY: That's like a French fairy tale I once read, "Riquet à la Houppe." It was about a hunchback and a beautiful princess.

MRS. MEDLOCK: So there is something that interests you.

MARY (*coldly*): I didn't say I was interested.

28. *Ext. roadway—dusk*

MRS. MEDLOCK: These are the moors.

MARY: The moors are ugly!

[MRS. MEDLOCK*'s patience is wearing thin, though she tries to cover.*]

MRS. MEDLOCK: Did your father ever tell you about Misselthwaite Manor?

MARY (*bitter*): Why should he? He didn't know he was going to die and I'd have to live there.

MRS. MEDLOCK: Very well . . . I will. Misselthwaite Manor is a grand place. It was built ages ago and has over one hundred rooms.

MARY (*caustic*): I don't care how many rooms there are.

MRS. MEDLOCK (*dryly*): Your manners could use improving.

MARY (*curt*): I don't have to be polite to servants.

MRS. MEDLOCK (*sharp*): Mind yourself, Missy. I'm Mr. Craven's housekeeper and servant to no one. I'll overlook your bad manners for now, seeing you've gone through so much sadness. Not that you'll find much joy at Misselthwaite Manor. Mr. Archibald still grieves for his wife and won't trouble himself with anyone.

29. Ext. Misselthwaite Manor—night
Various shots of the carriage as it approaches the main entrance of Misselthwaite Manor.

30. Ext. Misselthwaite Manor—night
As the carriage pulls into shot, JOHN, *a young footman, hurries out of the house.*

JOHN: Have a good trip, Mrs. Medlock?

MRS. MEDLOCK: I've had worse. Fetch Miss Mary's trunk. (*Stern*) And use the back stairs.

JOHN (*grinning*): I'll tiptoe all the way. Wouldn't want to wake the dead.

[MRS. MEDLOCK's *too tired to chastise* JOHN *for his flippant remark. She also knows what lies behind it.*]

31. Int. manor—entry hall—night
The hall, though richly furnished, has a cold, unlived-in look. Dimly lit, the tapestries on the walls recede into darkness. A staircase leads to the upper floors, and PITCHER, *an elderly, too-thin man, descends the stairs. He doesn't waste any time on amenities.*

PITCHER: You're to take her directly to her rooms. He doesn't want to see her, and he'll be leaving for London in the morning.

MRS. MEDLOCK: As long as I know what's expected of me, Mr. Pitcher.

PITCHER (*terse*): What's expected, Mrs. Medlock, is that you make certain Mr. Archibald is not disturbed and that he doesn't see what he doesn't want to see.

MRS. MEDLOCK (*dryly*): Well . . . there's a revelation. (*To* MARY) Come on.

[MARY *and* MRS. MEDLOCK *start up the stairs.*]

32. Int. bedroom—night
MARY *and* MRS. MEDLOCK *enter from the hall corridor.*

MRS. MEDLOCK: This is where you're going to live, Miss Mary. This is your bedroom, and the sitting room's just through there.

[MARY *makes no response.*]

MRS. MEDLOCK (*continuing*): The rooms were especially prepared for you.

[*Still no reaction from* MARY.]

MRS. MEDLOCK (*continuing*): I see a little supper has been laid out for you. You must be tired, so eat it and go to bed.

[MARY *looks at* MRS. MEDLOCK *with barely veiled contempt.* MRS. MEDLOCK *has had her fill of* MARY *for the moment.*]

MRS. MEDLOCK (*continuing*): Good night.

[MRS. MEDLOCK *moves to the door, opens it, pauses, then turns to* MARY. *She's grim now and her words carry a veiled threat.*]

MRS. MEDLOCK (*continuing*): You can go anywhere you like in this wing of the house, but you're not to go poking about anywhere else. Mr. Archibald won't have it and neither will I. Is that understood?

[*Over the eerie, disembodied sound of a child crying:*]

Cut to:

33. *Ext. the moors—night*
The pale moon, high in the sky now, illuminates the Martian-like landscape.

34. *Int. Mary's bedroom—night*
MARY, *lying awake in bed, suddenly hears the sound of a crying child. As the sound, filled with pain and despair, rises to a crescendo,* MARY *sits up and listens, obviously somewhat frightened.*

Fade Out.

Act Two

Fade In:

35. *Ext. the moors—dawn*

DICKON, *a boy of about twelve, sits near the moor path, fingering a panpipe. A crow is perched on* DICKON*'s shoulder, a little lamb snuggles against him, a small red fox lies at his feet, and a squirrel is nestled in his pocket. There's a sweetness about* DICKON*, a forever-innocence, yet we sense in him a wisdom that transcends time.*

DICKON (*beaming*): Mornin', Mr. Weatherstaff.

BEN: Mornin', Dickon. (*Teasing*) Wishin' the day in with a song?

DICKON: Just sayin' hello to the mornin'. (*Eager*) If you got a minute, I'll show you a trick I just learned.

BEN: I've work waitin' on me at the manor.

DICKON: Please . . .

[DICKON *looks disappointed.* BEN *hesitates. Despite his dour appearance and usually gruff manner,* BEN *is fond of* DICKON *and finds it hard to disappoint him.*]

BEN (*continuing*): Guess the work will wait till I get there.

[DICKON*'s delighted.*]

DICKON (*to crow*): Take yourself elsewhere, Soot.

[*The crow obligingly hops down from* DICKON*'s shoulder and settles on a rock.* DICKON *puts the panpipe in his mouth and plays a one-note "song" as he walks on his hands. He moves a few feet and falls over.*]

BEN (*laughing*): Good trick, especially the last part.

[DICKON *grins.*]

BEN (*continuing*): I'm off. See you around, Dickon.
DICKON: See you about, Mr. Weatherstaff.

36. *Ext. establishing shot—Misselthwaite Manor—day*

37. *Int. sitting room—day*
MARTHA, *a pretty, fresh-faced girl of about seventeen, wearing a starched white pinafore and a little ruffled cap, is setting out breakfast on the table. As MARY enters from the bedroom, MARTHA greets her with a warm smile.*

MARTHA: Mornin', miss.
MARY: Who are you?
MARTHA: Martha. Martha Sowerby.
MARY: Are you going to be my servant?
MARTHA (*amused*): I'm to do the cleanin' up here an' a bit of waitin' on you, though judgin' on your size, you won't need much waitin' on, will ya?
MARY (*curt*): Of course I'll need to be waited on. Someone has to dress me.
MARTHA (*confused*): Can you not dress yourself?
MARY: Of course I can, but in India my ayah dressed me!
MARTHA (*wry*): Well, you're in Yorkshire now, an' here children dress themselves soon's they're out of nappies. You'll find some lovely new garments in the cupboard, warm ones bought by Mrs. Medlock on Mr. Archibald's orders.
MARY (*sarcastic*): I thought he troubled himself with no one.
MARTHA: He don't. It was Mrs. Medlock who told him you'd not have proper clothing for the cold since you was comin' from India. An' it was she who had these rooms fixed up all pretty for ya. (*Kind*) I know you was wore out from your journey, so I hope you had a good sleep.
MARY (*caustic*): How could I sleep with all that crying and moaning. This is a haunted house, isn't it?

MARTHA (*flustered*): It was the wind you heard wutherin' across the moors. It often makes a mournful sound. You best eat your breakfast 'fore it gets cold.

MARY: I don't like English food.

MARTHA (*cajoling*): I've nine little brothers an' sisters who'd eat the table clean in a minute.

MARY (*startled*): Nine brothers and sisters?

MARTHA: No doubt there'd be more if my dad hadn't died in his prime. Feedin' that brood's hard on my mother, but Dickon's a help.

MARY: Who's Dickon?

MARTHA: He's one of our gaggle of children. He leaves what food there is for the others an' feeds hisself out on the moors. He says the wild goats give him their milk, an' there's lovely greens an' berries his for the takin'.

MARY (*dryly*): He sounds peculiar.

MARTHA (*laughing*): He's a rare boy, Dickon. He talks to animals an' they talk back.

MARY: That's the silliest thing I ever heard.

[MARTHA*'s enjoying herself too much to stop now.*]

MARTHA: And when he plays his panpipe, wild animals stop and listen.

MARY (*contemptuous*): Animals can't talk and they don't listen to music.

MARTHA (*teasing*): I told ya Dickon was a rare boy.

[MARTHA *starts toward the bedroom.*]

MARY (*curt*): I didn't dismiss you.

MARTHA (*innocently*): You'll be makin' your own bed up then.

MARY (*haughty*): You have my permission to go on with your work.

MARTHA (*admiring*): The Queen couldn't of said it better herself.

[*As* MARTHA *starts out:*]

MARY: I have nothing to do.

[MARTHA *reappears.*]

MARTHA: There's plenty of gardens you can go and play in, except for the one that's locked.
MARY (*sarcastic*): How can a garden be locked?
MARTHA: It can if there's a high wall 'round it. Dress warm if you're goin' out. March can be a cruel month in Yorkshire.

Cut to:

38. *Ext. vegetable garden—Ben Weatherstaff—day*
BEN *is using a shovel to break the still-frozen ground. A wheelbarrow and other garden tools are nearby.* MARY *comes into shot. She's wearing her new warm coat and matching bonnet.*

MARY: What are you doing?
BEN (*testy*): You got eyes. I'm turnin' the earth for plantin' vegetables when spring comes.
MARY (*haughty*): It doesn't surprise me you're rude. All the servants here seem to be rude.
BEN (*dryly*): I take it you're the little wench just come from India.
MARY: I'm not a little wench. I'm Mary Lennox, and you may call me Miss Mary, if you like. Where are the flower gardens?
BEN (*curt*): Other side, but naught blooms this time of year.
MARY: Where's the locked-up garden?
BEN (*glaring*): There's no door into it, so you can save yourself the trouble of lookin'!
MARY (*contemptuous*): Of course there's a door. If there wasn't, it wouldn't be locked.
BEN: Don't go pokin' your nose where it's no cause to go!
MARY: I think everyone in Yorkshire's mad as a hatter . . .

[*A robin sitting in a tree begins to chirp.* BEN *addresses the bird affectionately.*]

BEN: Ho, ho, you cheeky little beggar. Has you started courtin' this early in the season?

[*The robin chirps in response.* MARY'*s astounded.*]

MARY: He answered you!

BEN (*gruff, but pleased*): Considers hisself my friend.

MARY: I never had any friends.

BEN (*dryly*): Then we're a good deal alike, neither of us good-lookin' an' both as sour as we look.

[MARY *ignores the insult. For the first time she lowers her guard.*]

MARY (*wistfully*): Do you think he'd mind being my friend too? (*To the robin*) If you'll be my friend, I'll be yours.

BEN (*grudging*): You said that as nice an' human as Dickon talks to his wild creatures.

MARY: You know Dickon?

BEN: The very blackberries an' heatherbells know Dickon. The foxes show him where their cubs lie, an' the skylarks don't hide their nests from him. (*Embarrassed*) Off with you. I've work to do.

MARY: I think I shall look for the door into the locked garden.

BEN: All you'll find are rambles and thorns.

MARY: We shall see . . . shan't we?

[*A series of shots follows:* MARY *skipping along the moor, tossing a rock into the water;* MARY *walking slowly through various gardens;* MARY *sitting quietly next to the fire in her bedroom.*]

39. *Ext. the moors—day*

MARY *walks along the shore of the moors. Suddenly* MARY *spots* DICKON *and his animal friends.*

MARY: You're Dickon, aren't you?

DICKON: Aye. (*Smiles*) I was waitin' for you, Miss Mary.

MARY (*confused*): How do you know my name? And how did you know I was going to be here when I didn't know it myself?

DICKON (*matter-of-fact*): Sometimes wishin' makes things happen. (*Introducing his "creatures"*) The crow is Soot, the fox is Captain, the lamb is Lady, the squirrel is Nut. (*Grins*) The rabbit just happened to be passin'.

MARY: Those are strange names for animals.

DICKON: It's what they asked to be called.

MARY (*sarcastic*): Animals and birds can't talk.

DICKON: There's ways of talkin' that don't take words. (*Rising*) I've gathered some wild mustard seeds for Ben Weatherstaff, so if you don't mind company, I'll walk back to the manor with you . . .

[DICKON *pauses.*]

DICKON (*gently*): You're sad an' lonely now, but in time, you'll find happiness in Misselthwaite Manor.

MARY: No . . . I shall never be happy there! And I don't want your company nor anyone else's!

[MARY *moves off swiftly. She fights to hold back her tears, too proud to admit even to herself that she is lonely and unhappy.*]

Cut to:

40. *Int. sitting room—Mary—night*

The wind is howling. MARY, *in her nightgown, stands at the window looking out.* MARTHA *emerges from the bedroom.*

MARTHA (*cheerful*): Your bed's turned down an' the room's all cozy. Listen to that wind!

MARY: I looked for the door into the locked garden again today, but I couldn't find it.

MARTHA: Why trouble yourself when there's so many other gardens you can go and play in?

MARY: I like to know about things. Why was the garden locked up?

MARTHA (*sobering*): But for the garden, Mr. Archibald wouldn't be the way he is.

MARY: What do you mean?

[MARTHA *hesitates; then:*]

MARTHA: You'll not repeat what I tell you?

MARY: You know I've no one to talk to except you!

MARTHA: All right, then. But mind you, I'm only tellin' what Mrs. Medlock said 'cause this happened long before I came to work here. Mrs. Craven had that garden made when she first came to Misselthwaite as a bride. She an' Mr. Archibald would shut themselves inside for hours an' hours, like two lovebirds.

MARY: Well, if the garden was such a happy place, why was it locked up?

MARTHA: Because it's where the accident happened. There was an old tree in the garden with a high branch bent like a seat. Mrs. Craven—Lilias was her name— she loved to climb up an' sit on the branch an' read when she was alone. One day the branch broke an' she fell an' she was hurt so bad she died the next day.

MARY (*dramatically*): And Mr. Craven was so wild with grief that he locked up the garden and threw away the key!

MARTHA (*startled*): That's what Mrs. Medlock said, but how did you know?

MARY (*triumphantly*): I didn't, you just told me. And if there's a key, there must be a door, and I intend to find it . . .

[*Suddenly a great draft blows the door open. As* MARTHA *hurries to the door, for a fleeting moment we hear the sound of a crying child.* MARTHA *closes the door.*]

MARTHA: Someone must have left the door downstairs open to cause such a terrible draft!

MARY: You heard it, too, didn't you?

MARTHA: I heard what?

MARY: Someone crying.

MARTHA (*flustered*): I told you the wind often makes a mournful sound . . .

MARY (*coldly*): No, it wasn't the wind. It was human . . . and if it wasn't human, it was a ghost.

MARTHA (*nervous*): It was the wind you heard wutherin' across the moors. Good night, Miss Mary.

[*As* MARTHA *hurries to the door and exits,* MARY *looks after her, unconvinced.*]

Cut to:

41. Int. Mary's bedroom—Mary—night
MARY, *shaken, is sitting up in bed listening to the distant, heart-rending sound of a child crying.* MARY *gets out of bed, opens the door, and looks down the corridor.*

42. Int. corridor outside Mary's room—night
Dimly lit by a single gas lamp, the corridor stretches off into darkness. MRS. MEDLOCK *emerges out of the darkness. She's in her nightgown, a shawl over her shoulder. She hurries to the stairway and starts down.* MARY *steps into the corridor and listens, and the sound of a child crying grows louder.*

Cut to:

43. Ext. manor house—Dickon and Ben—day
BEN *sits at the base of a tree as* DICKON *approaches.* DICKON *hands a small napkin-covered basket to* BEN.

DICKON: Mornin', Mr. Weatherstaff. From my mother. She baked this mornin'.

[BEN *takes the napkin off, revealing a small loaf of bread.*]

BEN (*pleased*): My thanks to her. There's nobody bakes better bread than Susan Sowerby.
DICKON (*grinning*): She'll be pleased to hear it.

[DICKON *looks off. Sobers.* BEN *follows his gaze.*]

44. Ext. manor house—day—point of view—long shot—Mary
MARY *has just emerged from the manor and is moving away swiftly.*

45. Ext. manor house—day
DICKON *and* BEN *looking after* MARY.

BEN: There's not a day she don't go lookin' for the door into the locked garden, but she'll not find it. (*Bitter*) An' 'tis better so.
DICKON: Have you been in the garden, Mr. Weatherstaff?
BEN (*grim*): We'll not talk about that garden.
DICKON (*thoughtful*): Well, Miss Mary won't give up. There's a stubbornness in her, but there's also a need. I'm off. See you about, Mr. Weatherstaff.

46. Int. sitting room—day
MARY *stands at the window watching the rain come down in sheets.* MARTHA *is dusting the furniture.* MARY *turns to her.*

MARY: I've nothing to do when it rains.
MARTHA: Mrs. Medlock has wool to spare. You could knit.
MARY: I don't know how.
MARTHA: You could read.

MARY: I haven't any books.

MARTHA: There's thousands of books in Mr. Archibald's library.

MARY (*caustic*): Mrs. Medlock said I wasn't to go anywhere except in this wing.

MARTHA: The library's in this wing, but findin' it is a bit trickish, so I'll tell you how.

47. Int. portrait gallery—day

MARY *slowly enters the portrait gallery. The walls of the long gallery are hung with portraits of people long gone; men, women, and children in sixteenth- and seventeenth-century garb.* MARY *slowly looks up at the various portraits. The gallery interests her. She pauses, studies a portrait of a boy about twelve years old. He's a beautiful child with a pale, sensitive face and shock of black hair. He wears a velvet suit with a lace collar, the elegant apparel of seventeenth-century children. Intrigued,* MARY *studies the portrait for a long moment, then continues on.*

48. Int. Lilias's bedroom—day—Mary's point of view

MARY *enters the elegant bedroom. Maintained as though it were a shrine, the room is exquisitely feminine. The furniture is inlaid and the bed is draped in pastel silk. Gilt chairs are done in needlepoint. A rare Aubusson carpet covers the floor. A silk-draped dressing table is crowded with crystal perfume bottles. Against one wall, a tall, glass-fronted curio cabinet displays its treasures. Everywhere vases and bowls are filled with hothouse flowers.*

Entranced, MARY *moves slowly around the room. She pauses as she reaches the dressing table, picks up one of the perfume bottles, and shakes it. The bottle is empty.* MARY *takes the stopper out of the bottle and sniffs it. The scent still lingers.* MARY *seems shaken now. As she stares into the mirror remembering another time, another place:*

Flashback to Mary's parents' bedroom—(Delhi)—night
> MRS. LENNOX, *wearing a lacy peignoir, sits at her dressing table touching perfume to her throat and ears.* MARY, *in her nightgown, appears in the mirror behind her mother.* MARY *smiles, taking pride in her pretty mother. As* MRS. LENNOX *sees her in the mirror, she gestures impatiently that* MARY's *to go away.*

Lilias's bedroom—day
> MARY *stares at the mirror, hurt by the remembrance. As she replaces the perfume bottle, it clinks against another bottle and the sound triggers another memory:*

Flashback to dining room—(Delhi)—night
> CAPTAIN LENNOX, *his face damp with perspiration, his hand trembling, lowers his wineglass and it clinks against another glass.*

Lilias's bedroom—day
> MARY, *remembering, hurts for her father.*

Dissolve to:

49. Int. tapestry corridor—day
> *A ceiling-to-floor tapestry hangs on the wall at the end of the short corridor.* MARY *comes into shot. She pauses, aware she's reached a dead end.* MARY *freezes. The sound seems to be coming from behind the tapestry. As* MARY *moves slowly, nervously, toward the tapestry,* MRS. MEDLOCK *emerges from behind it. The shock is mutual. Then:*

MRS. MEDLOCK (*furious*): What are you doing here?!
MARY (*coldly*): You don't have to shout. I got lost going to the library. (*Looking at the tapestry*) I heard someone crying . . .
MRS. MEDLOCK: Old houses are full of strange sounds.
MARY (*softly*): I know what I heard, and it was someone crying.

[MRS. MEDLOCK, *aware* MARY'*s not to be put off, manages a smile of sorts.*]

MRS. MEDLOCK: Perhaps you're right. Betty, who works in the scullery, has been carrying on all day because she has a toothache. Come. I'll take you to your rooms.
MARY: Toothache?

Cut to:

50. *Int. manor—back stairs—Betty—day*
    BETTY, *a perky girl of about eighteen, carrying a breakfast tray, is going up the stairs.*

51. *Int. Mary's sitting room—day*
    MARY, *still in her nightgown, stands at the window looking out.* BETTY *enters.*

BETTY: Mornin', miss.
MARY: Who are you?
BETTY: Betty. It's Martha's free day an' she's gone to the cottage to give her mum a hand.

[*As* BETTY *starts to lay out* MARY'*s breakfast,* MRS. MEDLOCK *enters.*]

MARY (*dryly, to* BETTY): Is your toothache gone?
BETTY (*confused*): Toothache?
MARY (*too sweetly*): The toothache you didn't have.
MRS. MEDLOCK: Betty, cook wants you at the scullery.

[BETTY *takes the empty tray and hurries out.*

The exchange about BETTY'*s nonexistent toothache has made* MRS. MEDLOCK *somewhat uncomfortable. She manages a smile of sorts to cover.*]

MRS. MEDLOCK (*continuing*): It's terribly muddy out because of the rain. I thought we'd go into the village this morning and buy you a sturdier pair of shoes.

[MARY *studies* MRS. MEDLOCK, *her face expressionless.*]

MRS. MEDLOCK (*continuing*): It will be a nice little outing for you as well. I know you're lonely. When Mr. Archibald comes back, I shall speak to him. I'll ask him to get a governess for you.

MARY (*curt*): I had governesses in India. None of them stayed very long. They didn't like me.

MRS. MEDLOCK: Well, I'm sure that's not true.

MARY: Well, I don't lie, you do.

MRS. MEDLOCK: What a dreadful thing to say!

MARY: It's true! You lied to me yesterday about Betty having a toothache! There's something behind that tapestry and you don't want me to know about it.

[MARY *and* MRS. MEDLOCK *stare at one another.*]

Fade Out.

Act Three

Fade In:

52. *Ext. fountain garden—day*
MARY *is seen skipping rope in the garden, counting as she skips. She comes upon* BEN WEATHERSTAFF, *who is pruning trees.*

MARY (*proudly*): I only got the skipping rope from Martha last night and I'm already very good at it.
BEN (*dryly*): Maybe there's some child's blood in your veins after all.

[MARY's *too pleased with herself to take offense.*]

MARY: I have decided to skip one hundred times now without stopping.

[*As* MARY *skips away,* BEN *calls after her:*]

BEN: Pride goeth before a fall!

53. *Ext. path outside the secret garden*
MARY *skips into shot, counting aloud:*

MARY: Ninety-five, ninety-six, ninety-seven . . .

[*As* MARY *approaches the stone bench under the tree:*]

MARY (*counting; teasing*): Have you begun courting yet, you cheeky little beggar?

[*A robin is on the ground pecking at a small mound of dirt.*]

MARY (*counting; laughing*): Are you looking for food?

[*The robin flies off. The wind suddenly blows away the leaves from the ground and a small rusted ring protrudes from the mound.* MARY *picks up the ring; a rusted key*] *encrusted with dirt emerges.* MARY *brushes the dirt away. Stares at the key.*]

MARY: The key . . . (*Elated*) And if there's a key, there *must* be a door!

[*A sudden gust of wind hurls leaves into* MARY's *face. Looking up, she sees that the wind has separated the ivy surrounding the secret garden. Elated, she spots the door leading to the garden.* MARY *races to the door, pushes aside the ivy, and inserts the key. The door to the secret garden slowly opens and* MARY *sneaks inside.*]

54. *Ext. the secret garden—day*

Once inside, we see a "nightmare." The high walls are covered with dead ivy, and the thorny, leafless stems of dead rose vines are so thick they're matted. Dead brown grass chokes dead bushes. The branches of dead-looking trees are gaunt against the sky. Soggy leaves, the accumulation of years, form a spongy, rotting carpet. Everywhere, what were once climbing roses have spread and fastened themselves to trees and bushes, creating an ugly, thorny web. Stone urns that once held flowers are now filled with rotting debris. MARY *slowly, carefully walks around the garden when something suddenly catches her eye. A tiny green shoot has poked through the layers of dead rotting leaves. Camera pulls back to include* MARY *staring down at the shoot. It's the first living thing she's seen in the garden. She kneels and scoops the dead leaves away until the dead choking grass around the shoot is revealed.*

A dozen or so tender young shoots are now revealed. Camera pulls back to include MARY *looking down at the shoots.* MARY *smiles. In the midst of death, she has found life . . . minimal, fragile . . . but life.*

55. *Ext. secret garden path—garden door—day*

MARY *emerges from the garden. As she closes the door,*

pulling it firmly, a small piece of mortar falls from one of the bricks in the wall adjacent to the door.

MARY: It's my garden now. My own secret garden.

[MARY *tugs the brick and it comes loose. She's found a place to hide the key. She puts the key in the niche and replaces the brick. Then she pulls the ivy over the door and steps back to study the result. The door is now completely hidden again.*]

Cut to:

56. Int. sitting room—Mary and Martha—night

MARY, *in her long white nightdress, sits at the small table, eating her supper.* MARTHA *sits beside her.*

MARY: Is Dickon good at making things grow?

MARTHA (*laughing*): He can make things grow just by whisperin' to them.

MARY: When will it be spring?

MARTHA: Spring comes on sudden in Yorkshire. You'll wake up one mornin' an' the moors'll be all purple with heather. I'll go and turn down your bed now . . .

[As MARTHA *starts toward the bedroom:*]

MARY: I wish I had a little spade.

[MARTHA *pauses, surprised.*]

MARY (*casually*): If I had a spade, I could make a garden. (*Quickly*) A vegetable garden. I'd make it next to the big vegetable garden. It would give me something to do.

MARTHA: There's a little shop in Thwaite Village has garden sets for children, a spade an' rake an' fork all tied together, but it would cost two shillings.

MARY: Oh, I've got more than that. Much more. My mother always gave me money on my birthday so I could buy a present for myself, but I never did.

[MARTHA *barely manages to contain her anger at a mother who had so little interest in her child.*]

MARTHA: Well, if you give me the two shillings, I'll give it to the butcher boy when he comes an' he'll pass it on to Dickon. Dickon'll go and get your garden set for you.

[*As* MARTHA *goes into the bedroom,* MARY *looks after her, elated now. With the garden tools, she can accomplish much more in her secret garden.*]

57. Ext. secret garden path—day
DICKON *sits under the tree next to the bench playing his panpipe. The garden set, tied with a string, is on the ground beside him. As* MARY, *eager and filled with anticipation, hurries into shot,* DICKON *stops playing, picks up the garden set, and rises.*

DICKON (*beaming*): I've brought your garden set. If you'll show me where you want to make your garden, I'll be pleased to help you start it.

[MARY *hesitates. She hates lying, and there's a sweetness and openness about* DICKON *that makes it even more difficult.*]

MARY: If I tell you a secret, will you promise not to tell anyone else?
DICKON: Aye, if it's what you want.
MARY: I've stolen a garden.

[DICKON *looks confused.*]

MARY (*continuing*): I had to. It was locked up and no one's taken care of it for ages and ages and I'm not giving it back!
DICKON: A garden's not for givin' or takin'. A garden belongs to all. (*Studying* MARY) You found the door.

[MARY *nods.*]

DICKON (*continuing*): It was meant to be.

58. Ext. the secret garden—day
MARY *and* DICKON *enter the garden.*

MARY: I was hoping it would look different than before, but it doesn't. Everything still looks dead.

[DICKON's *eyes move over the garden.*]

DICKON: It's how I thought it'd be . . .

[DICKON *moves to a bush and snaps off a cutting. He shows the cutting to* MARY.]

DICKON (*continuing*): If you look deep, you'll see it still has a green heart. (*Looking around*) Could be others is wick, too.
MARY (*confused*): Wick?
DICKON: In Yorkshire, *wick* means 'live.
MARY: Even the thorny ones?!
DICKON: Aye. They've run wild an' attached themselves everywhere an' some will've died. But the strong ones will be wick, an' once the dead wood's cut away, there'll be roses.

[MARY's *eyes move over the "dead" garden. She's filled with wonder now, already visualizing the roses.*]

MARY: There'll be roses . . .

59. Int. sitting room—Mrs. Medlock—day
MRS. MEDLOCK *paces and* MARY *enters.*

MRS. MEDLOCK: Where have you been? Mr. Archibald is back and he wants to see you!

[MARY *tenses, fearful her guardian's discovered she's been inside the locked garden.*]

MARY (*almost afraid to ask*): Why? Why does he want to see me?

MRS. MEDLOCK: I imagine it's about the governess. I mentioned it to Mr. Pitcher and he said he'd pass it on to Mr. Archibald.

60. *Int. library—evening*

Ever so slowly, MARY *opens the door to the library and quietly enters. She walks farther into the room, staring at the beautiful overhead ceiling. She places her small hand on the arm of a chair. Suddenly an adult hand reaches out from the chair and clasps her hand.* MARY *jumps back in fright.* ARCHIBALD CRAVEN *slowly rises from the chair. He is tall and gaunt to the point of emaciation, and his black coat strains against the hump on his back. Though he's not yet forty, his dark hair is streaked with white. His skin is pale and chalky. Pain from a debilitating illness has etched his face with lines and created dark smudges under his eyes. A closer look would reveal fine, sensitive features.*

MARY *stands frozen, unable to take her eyes from* ARCHIBALD. *He beckons her.*

ARCHIBALD: Come here . . .

[MARY *stands rooted, unable to move.*]

ARCHIBALD (*continuing*): Don't be afraid. (*Bitter*) I know children usually find me frightening, but I'm quite harmless, I assure you.

[MARY *edges forward nervously.* ARCHIBALD *studies her.*]

ARCHIBALD (*continuing*): You're too thin . . .
MARY (*frantic*): I'm getting fatter!

[ARCHIBALD *continues to study* MARY. *Finally:*]

ARCHIBALD: You resemble your father. I only met him once, when we were boys, but I remember him. I envied him because he was on his way to Harrow and I was too ill to go away to school.

[ARCHIBALD *moves slowly to the fireplace. He holds his forehead.*]

ARCHIBALD (*continuing*): Ill. I have always been ill . . .

[MARY *manages to find her voice.*]

MARY: I'm sorry.
ARCHIBALD: Yes. Are they taking good care of you?

[MARY *looks away.* ARCHIBALD *moves to the winged chair next to the fireplace and seats himself.*]

ARCHIBALD (*continuing*): You find me repulsive, don't you?

[MARY *is shaken, but from somewhere inside herself she finds the courage to speak honestly.*]

MARY: You . . . you look different from other people . . . not repulsive.
ARCHIBALD (*bitter*): Different. Yes, I look different. If we met in the dark, would you scream and run away?

[*Again,* MARY *finds it impossible to be anything but honest.*]

MARY: I might, but it would only be because it was the first time.

[ARCHIBALD *manages a shadow of a smile.*]

ARCHIBALD: Honesty is rare. I value it. (*Beat*) Are you happy here?
MARY: I like India better.

[ARCHIBALD *stares into the fire. After a long moment:*]

ARCHIBALD: This is a sad house for a child . . . (*Beat*) We accept what we must. (*Beat*) Oh, I meant to get a governess for you, I forgot. I'll see to it now.

[MARY *tries to hide her distress. She doesn't want a governess. A governess would restrict her movements and she wouldn't be free to work in the secret garden.*]

MARY (*nervous*): Please, could I go without a governess for a while?

ARCHIBALD: Why?

[MARY *searches for a safe answer.*]

MARY: Well, I'm just getting used to being here. And when I came here, I wasn't very well . . . but now I'm getting better. And it's because I'm out a lot. And, well, if I had lessons, I wouldn't be out as much. And besides, I'm ahead on my studies. I know French, I'm good at history, and I read a lot.

ARCHIBALD: Very well. The governess can wait. Is there anything you need or want?

[ARCHIBALD *has given* MARY *an opportunity to ease her conscience about the secret garden.*]

MARY: Please, could I have a bit of earth to make a garden? I love gardens.

[ARCHIBALD *looks at* MARY *with shocked disbelief. Then he rises, moves to the window, and stands with his back to the room.* MARY's *shaken. She's upset, perhaps angered, her guardian and she doesn't know why. After a long moment,* ARCHIBALD *turns to* MARY. *Pain and grief are mirrored in his face. He finds it difficult to speak.*]

ARCHIBALD: There was once someone, someone very dear to me, who loved gardens, too. Take your bit of earth wherever you like. (*Turning back to the window*) Go now. Leave me . . .

[MARY *understands.*]

MARY (*whispers*): Thank you.

[*She hurries out of the room.* ARCHIBALD *watches her go, fighting to hold back his tears.*]

61. *Int. corridor outside library—day*

As MARY *moves into the corridor, she meets* MRS. MEDLOCK.

MRS. MEDLOCK: Miss Mary . . .

[MARY *simply stares up at her.*]

MRS. MEDLOCK: Well . . .

MARY: I think he's the saddest man I've ever seen, like the Hunchback of Notre Dame who died because he loved Esmeralda.

[MRS. MEDLOCK *looks at* MARY *with surprise. This is the first time she's heard* MARY *express concern or compassion for another.*]

Cut to:

62. *Int. Mary's bedroom—night*

MARY *stands by her nightstand, listening once again to the sound of the child crying. Though frightened, she is now determined to find the source of the weeping. Taking a candle, she steps out into the corridor.*

63. *Int. portrait gallery—night*

The pale light from MARY's *candle precedes her as she enters the gallery. In the wavering half-light, the portraits seem alive and menacing. A sudden clap of thunder followed by lightning frightens* MARY *even more. The crying of the child gets louder. The entire house is now filled with the menacing thunder and lightning.*

64. *Int. tapestry corridor—night*

The sound of weeping is close. MARY *appears at the top of the stairs. She looks toward the tapestry. A thin line of light is visible at the bottom of the tapestry. Suddenly the wind blows out the candle. Now, only the lightning is left to light up the corridor. Slowly,* MARY *inches toward the tapestry. Taking a moment to gather her courage, she pulls the tapestry aside and slowly moves inside.*

65. Int. Colin's bedroom—night

The large room is crowded with handsome old furniture. MARY's *eyes focus on the bed. The crying comes from someone rolling on the bed, covered by the bedcovers. Suddenly, the crying stops. Whoever is in the bed slowly drops the covers.* MARY *finds herself staring at a boy of about twelve. It is the boy who has been crying. As the boy sees* MARY, *he stares at her in shocked disbelief.* MARY, *equally shocked, stares back.*

Fade Out.

Act Four

Fade In:

66. *Int. Colin's bedroom—Mary and Colin—night*
For a long moment, MARY *and* COLIN *stare at each other. Then:*

COLIN (*frightened*): Are you a ghost?
MARY: No. I thought you were.

[*As* MARY *starts toward the bed:*]

COLIN: Stay away from me!
MARY (*continuing to the bed*): I'm Mary Lennox. I came here from India so Mr. Archibald Craven could be my guardian.
COLIN (*trembling*): Are you sure you're not a ghost?

[MARY *extends her hand as she moves to the side of the bed and sits.*]

MARY: Touch me. If I'm a ghost, your hand will go right through mine.

[COLIN's *hand trembles as it touches* MARY's.]

COLIN: You feel real . . .
MARY: I am. Who are you?
COLIN: Colin Craven. My father's master of Missel-thwaite Manor.
MARY: Your father?! Why didn't somebody tell me he had a son?!
COLIN: Because no one's allowed to talk to me!
MARY: Why?
COLIN: Because I won't have it . . . neither will my father.
MARY: Why?

COLIN: Because I'm going to have a hump on my back like he has!

MARY: Is that why you cry all the time?

COLIN: Yes.

MARY: Don't you ever go out of this room?

COLIN: No. If people look at me, I have a fit and get a fever.

MARY: I'm looking at you and you're not having a fit.

COLIN (*glaring*): I might.

MARY: Well, you can save yourself the trouble. Now that I know you're human, not a spirit or a ghost, I'm going back to bed.

COLIN (*imperious*): You'll stay. I've no one to talk to except my nurse, and she's away on holiday.

MARY: I don't have to stay if I don't want to.

COLIN: You said you came from India. I want to know about India.

MARY: You can read about India in books.

COLIN (*petulant*): Reading makes my head ache.

MARY (*tartly*): Well, if I were your father, I'd make you read so you could learn about things.

COLIN: No one can make me do anything!

MARY: Why not?

COLIN: Because I'm sick and I probably won't live to grow up!

MARY (*interested now*): Do you want to live?

[COLIN *bursts into tears.*]

COLIN: Not if I'm going to have a lump on my back like my father . . .

MARY: You are the cryingest boy I've ever seen! I'm going back to bed!

[COLIN's *so angry, he stops crying and glares at* MARY.]

COLIN: You'll stay till I say you can go!

MARY (*haughty*): You can't make me stay if I don't want to.
COLIN: Yes, I can! Everyone has to do as I say because I'm going to die!
MARY: People who always talk about dying are boring. I'm going.

[*As* MARY *starts toward the door,* COLIN *realizes he's met his match.*]

COLIN (*grandly*): You may go now, but you will come again tomorrow.
MARY (*shrugging*): I might if I don't have anything else to do.

[MARY *exits. Despite the heated exchange,* COLIN *is pleased and excited.* MARY *is his first contact with another child.*]

67. Int. Colin's bedroom—night
Angle on ceiling as a large shadow looms into view. The shadow belongs to ARCHIBALD, COLIN's *father.*

ARCHIBALD *stands next to the bed, looking down at his sleeping son. He grieves for* COLIN . . . *but there's bitterness as well.*

Cut to:

68. Int. Mary's bedroom—Mary and Martha—morning
MARY *sits on the bed tying her shoelaces.* MARTHA *is distraught.*

MARTHA: You shouldn't've done it, Miss Mary! You shouldn't've gone looking for Master Colin!
MARY (*tartly*): Well, if you'd told me Mr. Craven had a boy, I wouldn't have gone looking for who was crying.
MARTHA: But no one's allowed to talk about him or see him!
MARY (*dryly*): Then how do you know I saw him?
MARTHA: Because Master Colin told me! I'm the one has to look after him when his nurse is away.

[MARTHA's *on the verge of tears now.*]

MARTHA (*continuing*): I'll be blamed for tellin' you an' I'll lose my place here.
MARY (*impatient*): You won't lose your place because I won't tell anyone I saw him. No one's going to know except you.
MARTHA: But Master Colin said if you don't come now, he'll scream and scream till he brings the house down!
MARY (*outraged*): We'll see about that!

69. Int. Colin's room—day

COLIN (*furious*): You said you'd come!
MARY (*just as furious*): I said I might! Might is only *maybe*, and I don't care if you scream till you're blue in the face!

[COLIN *turns away. He looks so frail, so miserable,* MARY's *moved in spite of herself.*]

MARY (*continuing*): I suppose as long as I'm here I might as well stay.
COLIN (*eager now*): Bring a stool and sit next to me.

[MARY *moves to get the stool.*]

MARY: I never had to do anything for myself in India. English people are the lords and masters there, you know.
COLIN: No, I didn't know.
MARY (*dryly*): You don't know anything, do you?

[MARY *looks between* COLIN's *back and the pillows.*]

COLIN (*depressed*): You're trying to see the lump on my back, aren't you?
MARY: Bother your lump. I was just thinking how different you are from Dickon.
COLIN (*confused*): Dickon?

MARY: He's Martha's brother. If she wasn't so scared of you, she probably would have told you about him. Dickon's not like anyone in the world.

COLIN: Why?

MARY: Because he can charm animals and birds. He talks to them and they talk back.

COLIN (*overwhelmed*): That's magic.

MARY (*proudly*): Dickon's my friend, the first friend I've ever had.

COLIN (*imperious*): Then I shall order him to be my friend, too.

MARY (*contemptuous*): You don't know anything, do you? You can't order someone to be your friend. They have to want to be . . .

[*Suddenly,* MRS. MEDLOCK *and* DR. CRAVEN *enter.* MRS. MEDLOCK *is stunned, speechless, as she sees* MARY. DR. CRAVEN, *a tall, sensitive-looking man in his early forties, holds his medical bag. A gifted and dedicated physician, he barely manages to contain his anger now.*]

DR. CRAVEN (*to* MRS. MEDLOCK): How dare you permit a stranger in the sickroom?

[*Before* MRS. MEDLOCK *can defend herself:*]

COLIN: She's not a stranger and I want her here!

DR. CRAVEN (*stern*): Calm yourself, Master Colin. You know excitement makes you ill.

COLIN: You're the one who's making me so ill, so go away!

[*Though* DR. CRAVEN *is sensitive to* COLIN's *rudeness, his first concern is for his patient. A confrontation will do* COLIN *more harm than good.*]

DR. CRAVEN: You're to rest now. I insist. (*To* MRS. MEDLOCK) The vicar's ailing, so I'll get on to him and return tomorrow.

MRS. MEDLOCK: Yes, Doctor.

[MRS. MEDLOCK *looks back at* MARY *and* COLIN. *She is still shocked as she leaves the bedroom.*]

70. Int. kitchen—day
MRS. MEDLOCK *sits at the table drinking a cup of tea to settle her frazzled nerves.* BETTY *stands nearby.* MRS. GORDY, *the cook, a plump, middle-aged woman, looks dismayed.*

MRS. GORDY: So Miss Mary found our little tyrant . . .

MRS. MEDLOCK: Master Colin actually wanted her there.

BETTY: I always said what Master Colin needs is the company of another child.

MRS. GORDY (*tartly*): What Master Colin needs is a father who don't treat him like another plague that's been visited on him.

MRS. MEDLOCK: Anyway, it's done, and to tell the truth, I'm relieved in a way. It's been no easy thing trying to keep Miss Mary from finding out about Master Colin. Still, it's fortunate Mr. Archibald left for Cornwall this morning. Dr. Craven saw Miss Mary with Master Colin.

BETTY: He won't tell. He's Mr. Archibald's cousin an' down to inherit the manor someday, so he's not about to get Mr. Archibald angry.

MRS. MEDLOCK (*sharp*): We'll have none of that. I've known Dr. Craven since he and Mr. Archibald were boys. (*Continues*) It was seeing Mr. Archibald suffer that turned Dr. Craven to medicine. So you just watch yourself, my girl.

71. Ext. church—day
The church bells are pealing as parishioners stream out of the church. MRS. SOWERBY, *a motherly-looking woman in her forties, wearing a neat but shabby dress, walks from the church with two of her children.*

MRS. SOWERBY: Go and see what's keepin' your brothers and sisters.

[*As the older boy starts back toward the church,* MRS. MEDLOCK *approaches* MRS. SOWERBY.]

MRS. SOWERBY (*continuing warmly*): Mornin', Mrs. Medlock.

MRS. MEDLOCK: Good morning, Mrs. Sowerby.

MRS. SOWERBY: How's the little girl gettin' on, Mrs. Medlock? The one who come from India. (*To daughter*) Go and help your brother.

MRS. MEDLOCK (*grim*): There are times when her rudeness and arrogance make me wish she had never left India, but I'm sure Martha's told you that.

MRS. SOWERBY: My Martha don't gossip about what's goin' on up at the manor, though she did ask my advice about how to deal with the little girl.

MRS. MEDLOCK: I could use your advice, Mrs. Sowerby. After all, you have had ten children.

MRS. SOWERBY: No two are alike.

MRS. MEDLOCK: Yes, but even so.

MRS. SOWERBY: Well, then, if I'm not bein' too forward, I'll tell you what I told Martha. A firm hand is needed, but there's also the need to see what's behind it when a child acts up. From what Martha said, there's a lot of hurt inside the little girl. Seems to me, she's like one of those wild creatures my Dickon sometimes finds out on the moors caught in a snare or trap. It strikes out at Dickon whilst he's tryin' to help it, but in the end he wins their trust with his gentleness.

MRS. MEDLOCK (*politely*): The carriage is waiting, so I'll be running along. Good morning, Mrs. Sowerby.

[*As* MRS. MEDLOCK *moves off,* MRS. SOWERBY *looks after her. She knows that although* MRS. MEDLOCK *"got the message," she's not quite ready as yet to take* MARY *to her bosom.*]

72. *Ext. secret garden—day*

The garden glistens from a recent rain. Some of the dead branches on the trees and bushes have been cut away and lie in neat piles on the ground. MARY *and* DICKON, *holding hands, move quickly into the garden.*

MARY: How did you get so much done?! It's been raining for two days!

DICKON: I like the rain. So does the garden. Come, I've something to show you.

[*The daffodils, crocuses, and snowdrops have bloomed.*]

MARY (*joyfully*): They bloomed!

DICKON: Aye. Crocuses an' snowdrops an' daffydown-dillies is always the first to say spring's on the way.

MARY (*eager*): When will the roses bloom?

DICKON: Not till June.

MARY (*disappointed*): It's only the beginning of April. June's such a long way away.

DICKON: Aye, but when they bloom, there'll be curtains an' fountains of roses.

MARY (*overwhelmed*): Curtains and fountains of roses?

DICKON: Aye, but not unless the dead wood's cut away an' the earth is softened so it can drink in the rain. (*Surveying the garden*) There's lots to be done . . .

MARY: Well, tell me what you want me to do and I'll do it.

DICKON: If you'll clean out the flower urns, I'll bring fresh earth to put in 'em.

[*As* MARY *and* DICKON *move off, the camera moves with them.*]

MARY: I'm going to tell you another secret, Dickon. There's a sick boy who lives in Misselthwaite Manor and no one is allowed to see him, but I saw him.

DICKON: It's Master Colin you're talkin' about.

[MARY *pauses, astonished.*]

MARY: You know about him?

DICKON: Aye.

MARY: Did Martha tell you?

DICKON: My mother. Mrs. Craven fell from a tree an' the fall brought on her baby too soon. My mother knows midwifin', so she was called in to help the doctor with the birthin'. It was a miracle, my mother said, how Mrs. Craven held on to life long enough to bring her baby into the world.

73. *Ext. path outside secret garden—day*
DICKON *closes and locks the garden door, and the children move off.* MARY's *lost in thought.*

DICKON: You're still thinkin' about Master Colin . . .

MARY: He said he's going to have a lump on his back like his father and he'd rather be dead.

DICKON: I doubt he means that, though he probably wishes he'd never been born, an' that's just as bad.

MARY: Why?

DICKON: Those that feel unwanted scarce ever thrive.

MARY: I thrived and I didn't feel wanted. My mother didn't like me.

DICKON: Did you like yourself? It's where likin' has to begin.

MARY: I didn't like myself. I wasn't pretty, and I wanted to be because my mother only liked pretty things. Colin thinks he's ugly, too, and that's why his father can't bear to look at him and never comes to see him.

DICKON: Poor lad. There's not been much joy in his life. Have you told him about your secret garden?

MARY: No. (*Suddenly decisive*) But I'm going to, Dickon. It will give him something to think about besides feeling sorry for himself. (*Concerned*) What time do you think it is?

[DICKON *looks up at the sun.*]

DICKON: Well past three.

MARY: I've been out all day without stopping for lunch! Someone may be looking for me! (*As she runs*) Bring your animals tomorrow!

DICKON: If they don't want to play on the moors again, like today!

74. Int. manor house—entry hall—angle to Martha—day

MARTHA *is hurrying down the stairs as* MARY *runs up the stairs. In the background, we can hear* COLIN *shouting for* MARY.

MARTHA: Master Colin is causin' a terrible fuss 'cause you've not been to see him all day!

MARY: I don't have to see him if I don't want to!

MARTHA (*pleading*): Nurse Boggs is just back from her holiday an' has things to see to. You'd be doin' her a kindness.

75. Int. Colin's room—on Colin—day

COLIN *is pounding his bed and shouting.* MARY *is furious as she enters.*

COLIN: I waited and waited! Where were you all day?!

MARY: With Dickon.

COLIN: If you go to him instead of coming to me, I'll have him banished!

MARY: Who do you think you are, the Rajah of Punjab?!

COLIN: If you don't come, I'll have you dragged here! You're mean and selfish!

MARY: You're the one who's selfish! All you think about is yourself and feeling sorry for yourself!

COLIN: You'd feel sorry for yourself, too, if you had a lump on your back and you were going to die!

MARY: You say things like that because you want people to feel sorry for you!

[COLIN, *outraged, throws his pillow at* MARY.]

MARY (*continuing*): I was going to tell you something special . . . and now I'm not!
COLIN: I hate you!
MARY: Good! Now I don't have any reason to come and see you again, and I won't!

[MARY, *fuming, emerges from behind the tapestry. She runs right into* NURSE BOGGS, *who has been listening to the embattled children.*]

NURSE BOGGS: I'm Master Colin's nurse.
MARY (*sarcastic*): I feel sorry for you.
NURSE BOGGS (*wryly*): If he had a vixen of a sister like you, he might get well.
MARY: I don't care if he doesn't get well! If we were in India, I'd put a snake in his bed!

Fade Out.

Act Five

Fade In:

76. Int. Mary's sitting room—night
MARY, *in her nightgown and robe, sits on the floor in front of the fire, reading. At the sound of screams, hurrying feet, and slamming doors,* MARY *hurries to the door, opens it, and looks out.*

77. Int. corridor outside Mary's sitting room—night
NURSE BOGGS *is hurrying toward* MARY's *room.*

NURSE BOGGS (*agitated*): Master Colin's worked himself up into a terrible state and I can't calm him! I'm afraid he's going to do himself harm!

78. Int. Colin's room—Colin and Mrs. Medlock—night
COLIN *is screaming and struggling with* MRS. MEDLOCK, *who is trying to hold him down as he thrashes around the bed.* MARY *runs into the room and to the bed,* NURSE BOGGS *after her.*

MARY (*screaming at the top of her lungs*): Stop it, you nasty, hateful boy! It would be a good thing if everyone went away and let you scream yourself to death!

[COLIN's *so astounded he stops screaming.*]

MARY (*continuing; grim*): That's better. If you scream again, I'll scream, too, and I can scream much louder and longer than you can.
COLIN (*weeping*): I only screamed because I felt the lump on my back growing bigger.
MARY (*to* MRS. MEDLOCK): Can I feel the lump?

MRS. MEDLOCK (*horrified*): Certainly not!

COLIN: I want her to!

NURSE BOGGS (*grim*): Oh, let her, Mrs. Medlock, or there'll be no end to this.

MARY (*to* COLIN): Turn over.

> [COLIN *turns on his side,* MARY *draws her hand across and down* COLIN'*s back.*]

MARY (*continuing*): There's no lump.

COLIN: Yes, there is!

MARY: You've just got a knobby spine and knobby ribs like I have, so if you ever talk about lumps again, I'm going to laugh.

COLIN: I'm going to die!

MARY (*to* NURSE BOGGS): Is he?

NURSE BOGGS: The specialist from London said Master Colin would improve if he ate well and got out into the air.

COLIN (*to* MRS. MEDLOCK): You tell her!

MRS. MEDLOCK: You've been frail and sickly since you were born, Master Colin, and that's all I know. I've always hoped you'd outgrow your ailments, and I still hope. (*To* NURSE BOGGS) I'm worn out. Can you manage without me now?

COLIN: I want you to go! (*To* NURSE BOGGS) You, too! Only Mary can stay!

MRS. MEDLOCK: That's up to Miss Mary to decide.

COLIN (*pleading*): Will you stay with me, Mary? Please?

MARY: Well, since you said please. But if you scream again, I'll smother you with a pillow!

NURSE BOGGS (*sotto*): And she would, too.

MRS. MEDLOCK: Thank God Mr. Archibald's still away, or we'd be answering to him for this brouhah.

NURSE BOGGS: Thank God, indeed. I'd just as soon be spared this distressing business.

[MRS. MEDLOCK *and* NURSE BOGGS *exit.* COLIN, *exhausted from his tantrum, lies back on his pillow.*]

COLIN: You said you had something wonderful to tell me. Will you tell me now?

MARY (*tart*): You don't deserve to be told, but I will if you swear not to tell anyone else.

[COLIN *nods.*]

MARY (*continuing*): Nodding doesn't count.

COLIN: All right. I swear.

MARY: There's a secret garden and I've been in it.

COLIN (*confused*): A secret garden?

MARY: Yes. The door was hidden and it took me forever to find it, but I did. No one had taken care of it for so long that it became a wild tangle. Everything looked dead, but Dickon said some of the roses were still alive, and that when they bloomed, there'd be curtains and fountains of roses.

[COLIN'*s overwhelmed.*]

MARY (*continuing*): The first time I saw it, it was like an evil witch's garden, ugly and scary. But Dickon and I have worked and worked and now it's beginning to get beautiful.

[COLIN *tries to picture the garden in his mind's eye.*]

MARY (*fading*): Everything was gray, but now it's like a green veil hanging over the garden. A robin's made his nest there . . . in one of the trees. I call him "Beggar" . . .

[*Reaction shot of* COLIN *smiling brightly.*]

79. Ext. the secret garden—day

MARY *and* DICKON *are busily knocking away dead brush and logs.*

MARY: There are holy men in India called dervishes, who whirl and whirl until they go mad. That's what Colin was like last night.

DICKON: It's bein' lonely that makes him act like he does.

MARY: I was lonely in India, but I didn't have fits like that ... (*Continuing*) That's not true. If my ayah or governesses didn't do what I wanted, I'd have terrible fits. (*Sighs*) No wonder they didn't like me.

Cut to:

80. *Int. Colin's room—Colin—day*

COLIN, *propped up in bed, studies the pages of a large book filled with beautifully illustrated flowers. Under each flower is its Latin name.* MARY *enters and moves to the bed.*

MARY: I thought reading made your head ache.

COLIN: I'm just looking at the pictures. I told Nurse to get me a book with flowers, and she brought this one from the library. But I can't tell what the names are.

MARY: Flower books always use the Latin names.

COLIN: Do you know Latin?

MARY: No, but I know a poem that was first written in Latin. (*Beat*) "I do not love thee, Doctor Fell. The reason why I cannot tell. But this alone I know full well, I do not love thee, Doctor Fell."

COLIN (*delighted*): I like that. Do you know any other poems?

MARY: Oh, there are lots of other poetry books in your father's library.

COLIN: Will you read some of the poems to me?

MARY: I'll think about it.

COLIN: You smell nice.

MARY: It's the wind from the moors you smell. It's the springtime an' out-o-doors as smells so grandly.

COLIN (*confused*): I never heard you talk that way before.

MARY: I'm givin' thee a bit o' Yorkshire. (*Sternly*) Tha's a Yorkshire lad. Tha' should understand Yorkshire talk. It's a wonder tha's not ashamed o' thy face.

[COLIN *bursts into laughter.*]

MARY: Sometimes Dickon forgets and talks Yorkshire to me. I like it.
COLIN (*eager*): I'd like to hear him talk Yorkshire.
MARY: How can you if you don't want anyone to look at you?

[COLIN *stares at* MARY. *This is a big decision and it doesn't come easy. Then slowly, after a long moment:*]

COLIN: I don't think I'd mind if Dickon looked at me . . .
MARY: You mean that?
COLIN (*firmly now*): Yes. Yes.
MARY (*awed*): Well, wonders never cease.

Cut to:

81. *Int. Colin's room—day*
COLIN *is propped up on the sofa.* MARY *enters, followed by* DICKON. *They both carry* DICKON'*s animals.*

MARY: Colin . . . Dickon's here!
DICKON: I've brought along my creatures.

[DICKON *moves to sofa and puts the lamb in* COLIN'*s lap.*]

DICKON: Speak gentle and he'll take to you.

[COLIN *looks down at the lamb with wonder. Then he looks up at* DICKON *and smiles radiantly.* MARY *smiles, happy for* COLIN. *The protective wall she built around her emotions is coming down. As they pet the animals, all three youngsters smile broadly.*]

COLIN: The squirrel looks sleepy. I didn't know animals are so friendly, Dickon.

Cut to:

82. Ext. manor house—day

A wicker carriage chair (wheelchair) sits in the driveway. MARY *and* DICKON *walk up to the wheelchair, followed by* JOHN, *the footman, who is carrying* COLIN *in his arms.* NURSE BOGGS *and* MRS. MEDLOCK *follow behind* JOHN. *As* JOHN *sets* COLIN *in the wheelchair:*

COLIN (*glaring*): You hurt me!
MARY: Stop being such a crybaby!

[NURSE BOGGS *tucks the blanket around* COLIN.]

NURSE BOGGS (*firm*): This is your first time out, so it's to be only for an hour.
COLIN: It'll be for as long as I want! (*To* DICKON) Don't stand there like a stick! Push me!

[DICKON *moves off, pushing the carriage chair,* MARY *walking alongside.* MRS. MEDLOCK, NURSE BOGGS, *and* JOHN *look after the retreating children.*]

NURSE BOGGS: I'm all for it. It's wrong for the boy to be locked away like he wasn't fit to be seen.
MRS. MEDLOCK: Nurse is right, John. Master Colin can't spend his whole life in a world of his own making.
JOHN (*grim*): His making or his father's?
MRS. MEDLOCK: It comes to the same thing. (*Continuing*) One thing is sure. Mary Quite Contrary isn't about to take any guff from Master Colin.

83. Ext. driveway—day

The children come into shot, with DICKON *pushing the carriage chair.*

COLIN: All clear?
MARY: Safe as churches!
COLIN: I wasn't really yelling at you, Dickon . . .

MARY (*giggling*): We talked it over and decided if we were nasty, no one would get suspicious.

DICKON (*grinning*): Ah, I figured that out myself.

84. Ext. secret garden path— day
The children approach the secret garden. DICKON *is pushing the carriage chair slowly.*

COLIN (*impatient now*): Go faster, Dickon!

MARY: No! In case someone happens to see us, we don't want them to know we're going somewhere special!

85. Ext. secret garden path and doorway—day
DICKON *opens the door and* MARY *pushes the carriage chair through.*

86. Ext. the secret garden—day
It's April and the spring flowers have all bloomed: pink and lavender, yellow and white. The tender green of new ivy covers the high walls. Bushes and trees wear a "green veil." Though the roses haven't bloomed, the "curtains and fountains" are greening. The fruit trees are budding. Much still remains to be done—there's still wild growth and tangle— but the garden is already lovely. MARY *watches* COLIN, *waiting for his reaction.* COLIN'S *eyes move over the garden and his face lights up.*

COLIN: This is a magic garden. It will make me well and I will live forever and ever.

Cut to:

87. Int. scullery—Betty—night
BETTY *stands at the table polishing brass pots.* MARTHA *enters.*

MARTHA: I'm done turnin' down the beds, so I'll give you a hand if you like.

BETTY: I'm not about to say no.

[MARTHA *gets a towel and joins in the polishing.*]

MARTHA: Ya know, I was lookin' at Miss Mary tonight. She was all plain an' scrawny an' she's gettin' pretty.

BETTY: It's our Yorkshire rain. Makes the flowers an' children bloom.

MARTHA (*thoughtful*): She's changin' in other ways, too. She's still haughty sometimes, but not nearly as much.

BETTY: Her airs come from bein' spoiled when she lived in India.

MARTHA: I think it was the other way 'round. I think it was hurt and neglect made her act so badly.

BETTY (*teasing*): You're deep as a river an' twice as murky . . .

[JOHN *enters the scullery.*]

JOHN: Mr. Archibald's back.

BETTY (*tartly*): If you can't bring good news, don't bring any.

JOHN (*grinning*): Well, this'll cheer you. Mr. Pitcher said they'll be off again soon.

Montage:

88. *Ext. the secret garden—day*

MARY *picks some flowers from the now-blossoming garden. She trots over to* COLIN, *who is sitting cheerfully in his carriage chair, and hands him the flowers. He smiles broadly.*

DICKON *discovers a bluejay feather and runs over to show it to* COLIN *and* MARY. *He points to a tree, where we see a robin's nest with several newly hatched fledglings.* DICKON *happily tries to balance the feather on his nose.*

DICKON *and* MARY *are dueling with branch stocks.* MARY *runs off, and* DICKON *runs, trying to catch her.* COLIN *sits in his chair, smiling. The smile suddenly turns to a look of sorrow as* COLIN *realizes he is unable to run with the others.*

End montage.

89. Int. Colin's room—night
Moonlight streams into the room. COLIN *lies in bed, sleepless, unhappy because he can't be a part of* MARY *and* DICKON's *world.* COLIN *suddenly senses that someone has entered the room.* ARCHIBALD *enters and quietly moves to a covered portrait hanging on the wall. He pulls the cord, and the drape over the portrait parts. The portrait is one of Lilias Craven, an exquisite young woman.* ARCHIBALD *stares at the painting, agonizing over his loss. Slowly he closes the drapes again. As he exits,* ARCHIBALD *looks down at* COLIN *with a forlorn look on his face.* COLIN *buries his face in his pillow and begins to weep.*

90. Ext. driveway—day
ARCHIBALD *enters his carriage. The driver takes his seat up top.* MRS. MEDLOCK *walks to the carriage together with* PITCHER. PITCHER *is also dressed for traveling.*

MRS. MEDLOCK: Mr. Pitcher, did you find the sleeping powders?
PITCHER: Fortunately, or there'd be no rest for him tonight.
MRS. MEDLOCK: Any idea when you'll be returning?
PITCHER: It may be months. We're to travel on the Continent. Italy. Spain. Wherever.
MRS. MEDLOCK (*sighs*): He'd rather be anywhere than here.
PITCHER (*bitter*): With good reason. (*Glancing toward carriage*) The trunks are strapped. Good-bye, Mrs. Medlock.

MRS. MEDLOCK: Safe journey, Mr. Pitcher.

[MRS. MEDLOCK *looks on sadly as the carriage pulls away.*]

Cut to:

91. *Ext. the secret garden—day*
COLIN *sits in his chair watching* MARY *and* DICKON *working in the garden. He appears unhappy that he can't work with them.*

MARY: Do you think we'll ever get finished, Dickon?
DICKON: What's been left undone for years can't be done in weeks.
COLIN: I wish I could help . . .

[COLIN *turns away. He's close to tears and doesn't want* MARY *to see. Suddenly, he spots* BEN WEATHERSTAFF *at the top of the garden wall.*]

COLIN (*continuing; angry*): We're being spied on! (*To* BEN) Come in here!
MARY: He knows now. We'll be driven out like from the Garden of Eden . . .
DICKON (*to* BEN): This way . . . look at all the work we've done.
BEN: The hours you must have put in. I was up on the ladder . . . (*Turning to* COLIN) Poor crippled boy . . .
COLIN (*furious*): I'm not a poor crippled boy!

[*Holding the arms of the carriage chair,* COLIN *struggles to his feet, stands for a fraction of a moment, then falls back in the chair.*]

MARY (*numbly*): You stood up . . .
BEN: You're frail, but you're no cripple, an' you're not dimwitted . . .
COLIN (*outraged*): Who said I was dimwitted?

[BEN *pulls himself together.*]

BEN: Fools, that's who! But why've you locked yourself away . . .

COLIN: I thought I was going to have a lump on my back and my father hates me.

BEN (*distressed*): Your father doesn't hate you, Master Colin.

COLIN (*bitter*): Then why doesn't he come to see me except when he thinks I'm sleeping?

BEN (*gently*): Maybe it's because he wants to spare you his pain an' grief.

[COLIN *stares at* BEN; *then:*]

COLIN: I want you to promise me that you won't tell anyone else about our secret garden.

BEN: It was me that worked beside your mother to make the garden, an' I'll work again to make it like it once was.

MARY: You mean you'll help us?!

BEN: Aye.

COLIN (*defeated*): Now, I'm the only one who can't help.

DICKON (*to* MARY): Get the little spade an' the rose I potted this mornin'.

[MARY *understands what's in* DICKON's *mind and she smiles as she hurries away.* DICKON *lifts* COLIN *out of the carriage chair and puts him on the ground.*]

COLIN (*confused*): What are you doing? . . .

[MARY *hurries into shot. She gives* DICKON *the potted rose, then hands the spade to* COLIN.]

MARY: Dig a little hole. The earth's soft.

[COLIN's *confused, but he digs the little hole.* DICKON *shakes the plant out of the pot and hands the plant to* COLIN.]

DICKON: Hold it firm with one hand, push the earth around it, an' tamp it down.

[COLIN *follows the instructions, then looks up.*]

MARY: You just planted your first rose.

Cut to:

92. Int. Colin's room—day
COLIN *is propped up on the sofa, the doctor and* NURSE BOGGS *standing next to him.*

DR. CRAVEN (*concerned*): Nurse Boggs tells me you've been going out every day. You mustn't overdo, Master Colin.
COLIN (*curt*): I'll do as I please.

93. Int. tapestry corridor—day
The door to COLIN's *room is ajar, and* MARY *stands next to the tapestry waiting to go in.*

DR. CRAVEN'S VOICE: Your father has entrusted me with your care, Master Colin.
COLIN'S VOICE: Well, I don't trust you, so go away!
NURSE BOGGS'S VOICE (*distressed*): I'll see you out, Doctor . . .

[MARY *quickly presses herself into the corner next to the tapestry, reluctant to let the doctor and* NURSE BOGGS *know she's been eavesdropping.* DR. CRAVEN *and* NURSE BOGGS *emerge from behind the tapestry. As they move off:*]

DR. CRAVEN (*hopelessly*): Why does he dislike me so? I only want him to be well. It's all I've wanted since the day I brought him into the world and breathed life into him . . .

[MARY *looks at the doctor leaving, touched by his anguish. She runs back to* COLIN's *room.*]

94. Int. Colin's room—day

MARY: You're wrong about Dr. Craven. He wants you to get well. He wouldn't let you be so rude to him if you weren't such a poor, pitiful thing.

COLIN: I'm not a poor, pitiful thing! I stood up for a whole minute yesterday, didn't I?! (*Continues*) And from now on, I'm going to try to stand every day, and when I'm good at it, I'm going to try walking!

MARY (*sanguine*): It's about time.

Cut to:

95. Ext. the secret garden—day

MARY *and* DICKON *are supporting* COLIN *as he tries to walk.* COLIN's *feet drag uselessly on the ground.*

MARY: Pick up your feet, Colin! It won't work unless you pick up your feet!

COLIN: I'm trying!

MARY: Try harder.

COLIN: I'm tired. Take me back to my chair.

[MARY *and* DICKON *continue to half drag* COLIN *back to the carriage chair and ease him down.* BEN *watches the three youngsters in amazement.*]

DICKON: It comes hard 'cause your muscles are soft from not bein' used. We've a neighbor, Bob Haworth, whose legs was all spindly once, an' now he's a champion runner. Came from the exercises he done.

[COLIN *stares at* DICKON.]

COLIN: Could you show me how to do the exercises? Could you, Dickon?

DICKON: Aye! Give me your leg. Now push against me.

COLIN: Ow . . . that hurts, Dickon.

[MARY *looks at the birds' nest. The babies have grown bigger and* MARY *giggles in delight.*]

96. Ext. the secret garden—day
MARY *and* DICKON *are again supporting* COLIN *as he tries to walk.* COLIN *is obviously having a tough go of it.*

DICKON: Come on, Colin . . .

COLIN: Wait . . . wait . . . wait a minute.

[COLIN *slowly removes his arms from around* MARY *and* DICKON's *shoulders. He begins walking on his own—takes several steps and falls forward. In frustration,* COLIN *pounds the ground with his fists.* MARY *and* DICKON *rush over to him.*]

MARY: Stop . . . no, you can't get mad . . . you've got to try harder.

Fade Out.

Act Six

Fade In:

97. *Int. Colin's room—day*
COLIN *has taken to his bed again. He is withdrawn, detached. Camera pulls back to include* MARY, *standing next to the bed.*

MARY (*brightly*): It's nice out. You're not going to stay in bed all day, are you, Colin?

[COLIN *doesn't respond.*]

98. *Ext. the moors—day*
MARY *and* DICKON *walk slowly across the moor.*

MARY (*despondent*): Colin doesn't care any more if I come to see him or not. I don't know what to do, Dickon.

[DICKON *pauses. Looks off. He seems to be searching beyond this time and place. After a long moment:*]

DICKON: Colin'll find his way, an' you'll be the one that helps him find it. (*Smiles at* MARY) The way will come to you.

Cut to:

99. *Int. Colin's room—day*
NURSE BOGGS *helps* COLIN *into the chair.*

COLIN (*listless*): What're you doing . . . ?
MARY: We're just going to go up and down the corridors because it's raining and I don't have anything else to do.

[MARY *pushes* COLIN *out of the room.* NURSE BOGGS *looks after them.*]

NURSE BOGGS (*distressed*): He'd been doing so well . . .

100. *Int. portrait gallery—day*
> COLIN *sits looking at the portrait of the boy in the velvet suit.*

MARY: The boy in the picture looks like you. That's why I thought you were a ghost the first time I saw you. He's dead, of course, but you're alive.

> [COLIN *glances at the portrait, then turns away indifferently.*]

Dissolve to:

101. *Int. Lilias's bedroom—day*

COLIN (*whispers*): I smell roses . . .
MARY: This was your mother's room, Colin. She loved the secret garden, so she must have loved roses.

> [COLIN *looks up at* MARY. *His eyes fill.*]

MARY (*continuing*): Sometimes it's all right to cry, Colin . . .

102. *Int. Colin's room—day*
> MARY *has just drawn the drape over the fireplace open and is looking up at* LILIAS's *portrait.*

MARY: She's beautiful, Colin. As beautiful as a princess in a fairy tale. (*Turning to* COLIN) Why did you let your father cover your picture?
COLIN: I'm the one had it covered. I didn't want my mother to see the lump growing on my back.
MARY: Oh, Colin, she would've loved you even if you did have a lump. But I think she wants you to try to keep on walking, too.

103. Int. Colin's room—Colin—night

Moonlight illuminates the room and portrait. COLIN *lies in bed, looking at the portrait. The moments pass, then* COLIN *pushes his light covers aside and swings his legs over the side of the bed. Holding on to the nightstand, he stands. He releases his hold, takes a step, and he falls. He crawls to a chair and pulls himself up. Again and again, until he's soaked with perspiration, falling, pulling himself up, clinging to chairs and tables for support,* COLIN *struggles to walk until, finally, exhausted, he reaches the fireplace. Holding on to the mantle, he looks up at his mother's portrait.*

COLIN: Till I can walk, really walk, no one will know but you . . .

Cut to:

104. Ext. the secret garden—day

The roses have bloomed, a still wild but glorious profusion of pink, coral, and deep velvet red. DICKON *pushes* COLIN's *chair as* BEN *works in the garden.*

MARY: Well . . . the roses bloomed, even though it's been raining for days and days!

DICKON: They knew it was June.

BEN: Where you tend a rose, a thistle canna' grow.

[MARY *glances at* BEN *as though sensing something beyond his words.*]

105. Ext. outside garden—day

COLIN *sits in his chair with* MARY *at his side.*

MARY: I'm just thinking about what Ben Weatherstaff said about roses and thistles. He was talking about us.

COLIN (*confused*): About us?

MARY: Yes. Ugly thoughts are like thistles, and beautiful thoughts are like roses. As long as my head was filled with ugly thoughts, I didn't have room for pretty ones and I was mean all the time. As long as you thought about a lump growing on your back, you were nasty and rude.

[COLIN *considers this, then he smiles.*]

COLIN: Thistles and roses.
MARY: Thistles and roses.

Cut to:

106. *Ext. the secret garden—day*
It's July and the roses and summer flowers are in full bloom. BEN *and* DICKON *look around, admiring the fruits of their hard work.* MARY *walks over to* COLIN, *who is seated in his chair. She carries the fox in her arms and sings.*

MARY (*singing*):
"She is coming, my dove, my dear;
She is coming, my life, my fate . . .
The red rose cries, she is near.
She is near, and the white rose weeps, she is late."

Cut to:

107. *Int. Colin's room—night*
COLIN *lies on the bed.* MARY *sits next to him and continues to sing.*

MARY (*singing*):
"The larkspur listens
I hear, I hear . . . "
COLIN (*whispering*):
"And the lily whispers, I wait."

[COLIN *and* MARY *smile at one another.*]

Cut to:

108. *Ext. the secret garden—day*
COLIN *sits in his chair with* MARY, DICKON, *and* BEN *standing nearby.*

COLIN: Come here, everyone . . . hurry up . . . come on. I have an announcement to make. I have decided that when I grow up, I am going to do important experiments with magic. (*To* MARY) You know a little bit about magic because you grew up in India, where there are fakirs. (*To* DICKON) You can charm animals, so you know some magic, too. (*Beat*) I am now going to show you my first magic experiment.

> [COLIN *rises from the carriage chair. As* MARY, DICKON, *and* BEN *watch, astounded,* COLIN, *though somewhat unsteady, walks a few feet to a flower bush, picks a flower, brings it to* MARY, *then sinks down in his chair, tired but triumphant.*]

COLIN (*continuing*): That is my first experiment!
MARY (*numb*): You walked. You walked all by yourself . . .
COLIN (*elated*): I've been practicing! Every night after Nurse Boggs went to bed, I practiced!

> [DICKON *smiles.* BEN's *eyes fill.*]

BEN: Praise God . . .

> [*Unnoticed,* MRS. SOWERBY *has entered the garden.*]

MRS. SOWERBY (*overcome by emotion*): Amen.
DICKON (*to his mother, wryly*): You're in, so you might as well come all the way . . .

> [*As* MRS. SOWERBY *moves forward:*]

MRS. SOWERBY: I was passin' an' heard voices, but never did I envision what I just saw—Master Colin up an' walkin'!
DICKON (*to* COLIN): No cause to worry. She's my mother, Susan Sowerby.
COLIN: Since you're Dickon's mother, I guess I don't mind your knowing I can walk now. I don't want anyone else to know.

BEN (*dismayed*): Surely, you want your father to know.

COLIN: Not yet. I want to surprise him. When he comes home, I shall walk to him and say, "I can walk now, Father, and I shall grow up and make you proud of me!" (*Firmly*) It has to be that way. That's part of the magic.

BEN (*moved*): I never knew it by that name, but what does a name matter? Call it magic or a miracle or the touch of God's hand . . .

MRS. SOWERBY (*loving*): It's the Good Big Thing, Master Colin, an' I hope you'll never stop believin' in it.

MARY: Oh, he won't.

[DICKON *smiles.*]

Cut to:

109. *Int. Colin's room—night*

NURSE BOGGS *is turning down the bed.* COLIN *is propped on the sofa.* MARY *sits on the low stool beside him, books scattered on the floor around her.* NURSE BOGGS *finishes and moves toward the door.*

NURSE BOGGS: I'll be back in a little while to put you to bed, Master Colin.

[NURSE BOGGS *exits.*]

COLIN (*worried*): I hope Dr. Craven isn't getting suspicious. When he was here before, he noticed my legs look stronger and that I'm getting fatter. (*Hoping*) Maybe he'll think I'm bloated. Sick people get bloated, don't they?

MARY: Dead people get bloated when they're left out in the sun. I once saw a dead beggar in India who was so bloated he looked like a melon about to burst.

COLIN: I don't like to talk about dead people or dying.

MARY: I know, but you used to. You're not rude to Dr. Craven anymore, either.

COLIN: I know. I used to think he wanted me to die, and now I know he doesn't. (*Hesitates*) Mary, do you like

Dickon more than you like me? (*Quickly*) I don't mind if you like Dickon. I just want you to like me, too.
MARY: I like you the same but different.

Cut to:

110. *Ext. the secret garden—angle to Dickon—day*
DICKON *marches around the garden, playing his panpipe. Soot is on his shoulder, the squirrel peeps out of his pocket.*

MARY *and* COLIN *sit under a tree watching* DICKON, *delighted with the "performance."* COLIN *suddenly reaches into his pocket.*

COLIN (*suddenly shy*): I have a present for you.

[COLIN *takes a small velvet box out of his pocket, hands it to* MARY, *and she opens it. Inside the box is a small heart-shaped locket suspended from a thin gold chain.* MARY *is absolutely astonished.*]

MARY: Oh, Colin . . . it's beautiful.
COLIN (*proudly*): I picked it out myself from a catalogue, and Mrs. Medlock ordered it for me all the way from London.

[MARY *puts the locket on.*]

MARY: I shall wear it always.

[COLIN *smiles and* MARY *responds. Though neither fully understands, both seem to sense they've made a commitment to each other.*]

Cut to:

111. *Ext. sanitarium—day*
ARCHIBALD *is asleep on a lounge, covered with a blanket. Several medicine bottles, a water carafe, and a glass are on the low table beside the lounge.* ARCHIBALD *stirs in his*

sleep. He dreams. The picture distorts, and as though through a clouded mirror, we share his dream:

112. Ext. secret garden—day

We see LILIAS *standing in the garden.* LILIAS *is lovely in her airy white dress.* ARCHIBALD *takes her in his arms and they're lost in a kiss. Then* LILIAS *frees herself, smiles, and moves off. She pauses abruptly and turns to* ARCHIBALD, *deeply troubled now. The picture distorts. When it comes into focus:*

113. Ext. sanitarium balcony—day

ARCHIBALD *is suddenly awakened by the sound of* PITCHER *calling to him. He holds a letter in his hand.*

PITCHER: It's time for your medicine, Mr. Archibald. Also, this letter just arrived from your solicitor. Shall I see what it is?

[ARCHIBALD *nods, still caught up in his dream.* PITCHER *opens the envelope and takes out a smaller envelope.*]

PITCHER (*continuing; confused*): Another letter is enclosed. Shall I read it?

[ARCHIBALD *nods indifferently.* PITCHER *takes the letter out of the envelope, puts on his spectacles, then reads:*]

PITCHER (*continuing; reading*): "Dear Sir: I am Susan Sowerby who is Martha's mother who works for you in Misselthwaite Manor. I am making bold to speak to you. Please sir, I would come home if I were you. I think you would be glad you came, and if you will excuse me sir, I think your lady would want you to come if she were here. Your obedient servant, Susan Sowerby."

[ARCHIBALD *stares at* PITCHER *in shocked disbelief.*]

PITCHER (*continuing; frightened*): What is it?

ARCHIBALD (*whispers*): I dreamed of Lilias . . .

Cut to:

114. *Ext. the secret garden—day*
Summer is drawing to a close. Petals from the overblown roses are scattered on the ground. COLIN *sits cheerfully in his carriage chair as* MARY *picks some flowers.*

DICKON: I've an errand to run, so I'm off to Thwaite Village now.

COLIN (*concerned*): You'll come back, won't you? You have to push me back to the house.

DICKON: Aye, I'll be back. (*Teasing*) The game's not played out yet.

COLIN (*laughing*): I like that. The game's not played out. I'm glad you're my friend, Dickon. You'll always be my friend, won't you?

[*For a fleeting moment, a shadow falls across* DICKON's *face, as though the sun's gone behind a cloud.*]

DICKON (*quietly*): We'll be parted, you an' me, but remembrance will keep us friends.

[DICKON *exits.*]

COLIN (*frowning*): Mary, why did Dickon say we'd be parted? How can he know that?

MARY: Dickon knows things no one else knows.

[COLIN *gets up from the carriage chair and walks with* MARY *through the garden. As they circle the garden,* MARY *looks at the overblown roses with regret.*]

MARY: Summer's almost over.

COLIN: I know. What will we do all winter, Mary?

MARY: We'll probably go to school. We're both too old for governesses, and you're well now.

COLIN (*hoping*): Perhaps we can go to the same school.

MARY: No. Girls go to girls' schools and boys to boys'.

COLIN: I suppose there's no help for it.

MARY: You better sit down for a bit . . .

[COLIN *seats himself in the carriage chair.*]

COLIN: I wish we didn't have to go to different schools . . .

MARY: We'll write letters to each other.

COLIN (*disconsolate*): But it won't be the same. And we won't be able to come to our secret garden.

MARY: Oh, our garden will be here when we come back. And while we're away, we can think about how beautiful it is. And how it's waiting for us.

[*Suddenly* ARCHIBALD *walks into the garden. His eyes are fixed on* COLIN *with stunned disbelief.* MARY, COLIN, *and* ARCHIBALD *are frozen in place. Immobilized. The shock is mutual.* ARCHIBALD's *eyes fill.*]

ARCHIBALD (*whispers*): Colin . . . son . . .

[COLIN *stares at his father. This is the moment he's been waiting for, and he's rigid. Unable to move.* MARY *whispers to* COLIN.]

MARY (*desperately*): Get up. Get up and walk! Come on, you know you can do it.

[COLIN *remains rigid, his eyes fixed on his father.*]

MARY (*continuing*): You know you can. Please, Colin . . . go. Come on, go.

[COLIN *stirs. Then slowly, his eyes fixed on his father,* COLIN *rises out of the carriage chair. As* COLIN *moves slowly, tentatively, toward his father,* ARCHIBALD *is overcome with emotion. Weeping tears of joy, he opens his arms to receive* COLIN. *Enfolds him.*]

ARCHIBALD (*weeping*): My boy . . . my son . . .

COLIN: Don't cry, Father. I'm well now! I can walk, and I'm going to live forever!

[MARY *smiles in delight.*]

COLIN (*continuing*): It was the secret garden that made me well, Father. My mother's garden. And it was Mary who made me walk.

[MARY *walks over to* ARCHIBALD. *He clasps her hand in appreciation.*]

ARCHIBALD (*to* MARY): Thank you.

COLIN: Come see our garden.

[*Hand in hand,* ARCHIBALD *and the two youngsters begin to stroll through the garden.*]

Cut to:

115. *Ext. vegetable garden—day (1918)*
MARY, *the lovely young woman in the Red Cross uniform, is seated on a bench under a tree. Suddenly, a gnarled hand reaches out and touches her shoulder. She turns, rises, and embraces* BEN WEATHERSTAFF.

MARY: Ben! Ben Weatherstaff!

[BEN *holds out the rusted key for the secret garden.*]

BEN: You'll be needin' this to unlock the garden.

MARY (*overjoyed*): Ben, it's been so long!

BEN: I didn't know you, you've changed so . . .

MARY (*laughing*): I grew up.

[*A shadow crosses* BEN's *face.*]

BEN (*somber*): You know about Dickon?

MARY: Mrs. Medlock wrote to me. She wrote with such love. Such compassion.

BEN: You touched her heart an' warmed it . . . (*Heavily*) Killed in the war. Dickon. In a forest called the Argonne . . .

MARY: If Dickon had to die, he would have chosen a place where there were green and growing things.

BEN: Aye. But to die so young. Who was to know . . .

MARY (*gently*): Dickon knew.

BEN (*managing a smile while fighting back tears*): Aye. Dickon knew. Come. I'll unlock the garden for you.

116. Ext. the secret garden—day

The garden is as we have never seen it before, a mystical and magical place. Roses cascade like waterfalls. Bushes have been transformed into the exquisite forms of woodland creatures. Low-growing flowers are a pink and lavender carpet. Lilies are massed against the walls and the walls are covered with tender green ivy. Pastel flowers tumble out of the stone urns. A little stream meanders through the garden; violets grow in the damp and shadowed crevices of the lichen-covered rocks that border it. MARY *is filled with wonder, beyond words. Finally:*

MARY: I dreamed about the garden, but even in my dreams, it was never this beautiful . . .

[MARY *smiles tremulously at* BEN.]

MARY (*continuing*): You did it, Ben. All these years . . .

BEN: There was a promise to be kept. As Mr. Archibald lay dyin', he said to me, "Tend the garden, Ben. Someday the children'll be comin' back, an' when they do, their garden must be a magic place . . ."

MARY (*loving*): And it is.

MAN'S VOICE (COLIN): Where you tend a rose, a thistle cannot grow . . .

[MARY *wheels toward the door.*]

MARY (*joyful*): Colin!

[COLIN *stands in the garden door. Twenty-five now,* COLIN *is tall and handsome. He wears the uniform of a British officer and is leaning on a cane.* MARY *moves to* COLIN; *they embrace and kiss.*]

MARY: I wasn't sure the hospital would release you!
COLIN (*teasing*): Did you think I'd let a little shrapnel stop me?

[COLIN *studies* MARY, *sober now.*]

COLIN (*continuing*): When I was at Oxford, I asked you to marry me. When I was in France, I wrote and asked you to marry me. Why wouldn't you give me an answer, Mary?
MARY: I wanted you to ask me here, in our garden.

[COLIN *looks at* MARY *with love.*]

COLIN: I should have known. Will you marry me, Mary Lennox?
MARY: Of course.

[MARY *and* COLIN *join hands and stroll in the garden as* BEN *moves forward to congratulate them both. Camera pulls back as the three of them enjoy the sights and memories of the secret garden.*]

Frances Hodgson Burnett
(1849–1924)

Readers of *The Secret Garden* probably won't be surprised to learn that Frances Hodgson Burnett loved gardening. She even enjoyed weeding. In her last book, *In the Garden,* published after her death, she wrote: "I love to dig. I love to kneel down on the grass at the edge of a flower bed and pull out the weeds fiercely and throw them into a heap by my side. . . . And when at last . . . it seems as if I had beaten them, . . . I go away feeling like an army with banners."

Frances Hodgson Burnett was an unusual woman for her time. In an era when most women depended on men for financial support, she worked hard at the writing career that made her rich and famous. She did most of her writing in the late 1800s, but her best novel, *The Secret Garden,* was written at the beginning of the twentieth century, in 1909. Burnett's biggest success during her lifetime was her first novel written for children, *Little Lord Fauntleroy* (1886). That story, about a poor American boy who inherits his noble father's title, seems old-fashioned now. In *A Little Princess* (1905), a poor orphan from India goes to live in a boarding school in London. New movies of both *The Secret Garden* and *A Little Princess* have been made within the past ten years.

Frances Hodgson was born in the manufacturing town of Manchester, England. Her family was wealthy, but after her father's death, when Frances was four years old, the family's furniture business fell on hard times. The Hodgsons moved to a working-class neighborhood where their mother struggled to keep them out of poverty. The five children were not allowed to play with mill-workers' children, but in her autobiography, *The One I Knew the Best of All*, Frances Hodgson Burnett recalls that she loved listening to the broad dialect spoken by "street children." Much of her writing, including *The Secret Garden*, reveals the knowledge of dialect that she picked up as a child.

When she was sixteen, the Hodgson family emigrated to Knoxville, Tennessee. They expected to improve their financial situation, but Knoxville in 1865, just after the Civil War, was a sad place, with ruined houses everywhere. There was work for just one brother, and even that job didn't last long. Moving to the small village of New Market, the family lived in a crowded log cabin. They were extremely poor, often without enough money for food or a fire.

Two years after the move to Tennessee, Frances, desperate to earn money, sold her first story to a magazine. She was paid twenty dollars, more than most men in those days made in a month. After that, she never stopped supporting her family by writing. In the late Victorian era, Frances Hodgson Burnett was considered a highly independent woman. Some critics estimate that she made more money from writing than any other author of her time.

Burnett wrote short stories, novels, and plays for adults and children. Writing wasn't always easy for her. She sometimes complained that she felt like "a pen-driving machine, warranted not to wear out." But she always found comfort and happiness in making gardens. "As long as one has a garden," she wrote, "one has a future."

Pyramus and Thisby

William Shakespeare

Characters

Peter Quince, a carpenter, the director of the play, who also delivers the Prologue

Nick Bottom, a weaver, who takes the part of the lover Pyramus

Francis Flute, a bellows-mender, who takes the part of Thisby

Robin Starveling, a tailor, who presents Moonshine

Tom Snout, a tinker, who plays the Wall

Snug, a joiner, or cabinetmaker, who plays the Lion

Theseus (thē´sē-əs), Duke of Athens

Hippolyta (hi-pol´i-tə), queen of the Amazons and bride of Theseus

Philostrate (fī´lō-strä´tē), master of the revels

Courtiers, Ladies, and Attendants

Scene 1

QUINCE's *house. Enter* QUINCE, SNUG, BOTTOM, FLUTE, SNOUT, *and* STARVELING.

Quince. Is all our company here?

Bottom. You were best to call them generally,[1] man by man, according to the scrip.[2]

---

1. **generally:** Bottom means "severally" or "separately."
2. **scrip:** list.

Quince. Here is the scroll of every man's name which is thought fit, through all Athens, to play in our interlude[3] before the Duke and the Duchess on his wedding day at night.

Bottom. First, good Peter Quince, say what the play treats on. Then read the names of the actors, and so grow to a point.[4]

Quince. Marry,[5] our play is *The most lamentable comedy and most cruel death of Pyramus and Thisby.*

Bottom. A very good piece of work, I assure you, and a merry. Now, good Peter Quince, call forth your actors by the scroll. Masters, spread yourselves.

Quince. Answer as I call you. Nick Bottom, the weaver.

Bottom. Ready. Name what part I am for, and proceed.

Quince. You, Nick Bottom, are set down for Pyramus.

Bottom. What is Pyramus? A lover, or a tyrant?

Quince. A lover, that kills himself most gallant for love.

Bottom. That will ask some tears in the true performing of it. If I do it, let the audience look to their eyes, I will move storms, I will condole[6] in some measure. To the rest. Yet my chief humor[7] is for a tyrant. I could play Ercles[8] rarely, or a part to tear a cat in,[9] to make all split.

"The raging rocks
And shivering shocks
Shall break the locks
    Of prison gates.
And Phibbus' car[10]

---

3. **interlude:** play.
4. **grow to a point:** conclude.
5. **Marry:** an exclamation.
6. **condole:** Bottom means "lament."
7. **humor:** whim.
8. **Ercles:** Hercules.
9. **tear a cat in:** to overact.
10. **Phibbus' car:** the chariot of Phoebus, the sun god.

> Shall shine from far,
>   And make and mar
>   The foolish Fates."

This was lofty! Now name the rest of the players. This is Ercles' vein, a tyrant's vein.[11] A lover is more condoling.

Quince. Francis Flute, the bellows-mender.

Flute. Here, Peter Quince.

Quince. Flute, you must take Thisby on you.

Flute. What is Thisby? A wandering knight?

Quince. It is the lady that Pyramus must love.

Flute. Nay, faith, let not me play a woman. I have a beard coming.

Quince. That's all one. You shall play it in a mask, and you may speak as small[12] as you will.

Bottom. An[13] I may hide my face, let me play Thisby too. I'll speak in a monstrous little voice, "Thisne, Thisne." "Ah Pyramus, my lover dear! Thy Thisby dear, and lady dear!"

Quince. No, no. You must play Pyramus, and Flute, you Thisby.

Bottom. Well, proceed.

Quince. Robin Starveling, the tailor.

Starveling. Here, Peter Quince.

Quince. Robin Starveling, you must play Thisby's mother. Tom Snout, the tinker.

Snout. Here, Peter Quince.

Quince. You, Pyramus' father. Myself, Thisby's father. Snug, the joiner, you, the lion's part. And, I hope, here is a play fitted.

---

11. **tyrant's vein:** In ancient drama, Hercules was portrayed as a ranting character.
12. **small:** shrilly.
13. **an:** if.

Snug. Have you the lion's part written? Pray you, if it be, give it me, for I am slow of study.

Quince. You may do it extempore, for it is nothing but roaring.

Bottom. Let me play the lion too. I will roar that I will do any man's heart good to hear me; I will roar that I will make the Duke say, "Let him roar again, let him roar again."

Quince. An you should do it too terribly, you would fright the Duchess and the ladies, that they would shriek; and that were enough to hang us all.

All. That would hang us, every mother's son.

Bottom. I grant you, friends, if you should fright the ladies out of their wits, they would have no more discretion but to hang us. But I will aggravate[14] my voice so that I will roar you as gently as any sucking dove, I will roar you an 'twere any nightingale.

Quince. You can play no part but Pyramus; for Pyramus is a sweet-faced man, a proper[15] man as one shall see in a summer's day, a most lovely, gentlemanlike man. Therefore you must needs play Pyramus.

Bottom. Well, I will undertake it. What beard were I best to play it in?

Quince. Why, what you will.

Bottom. I will discharge it in either your straw-color beard, your orange-tawny beard, your purple-in-grain[16] beard, or your French-crown-color beard, your perfect yellow.

Quince. Masters, here are your parts. And I am to entreat you, request you, and desire you, to con[17] them by

---

14. **aggravate:** Bottom means "restrain."
15. **proper:** handsome.
16. **purple-in-grain:** dyed purple.
17. **con:** learn.

tomorrow night; and meet me in the palace wood, a mile without the town, by moonlight. There will we rehearse, for if we meet in the city, we shall be dogged with company, and our devices known. In the meantime I will draw a bill of properties such as our play wants. I pray you, fail me not.

Bottom. We will meet, and there we may rehearse most obscenely[18] and courageously. Take pains, be perfect. Adieu.

Quince. At the Duke's Oak we meet.

Scene 2

A wood near Athens. Enter QUINCE, SNUG, BOTTOM, FLUTE, SNOUT, *and* STARVELING.

Bottom. Are we all met?

Quince. Pat,[19] pat, and here's a marvelous convenient place for our rehearsal. This green plot shall be our stage, this hawthorn brake[20] our tiring-house;[21] and we will do it in action as we will do it before the Duke.

Bottom. Peter Quince—

Quince. What sayest thou, bully Bottom?

Bottom. There are things in this comedy of Pyramus and Thisby that will never please. First, Pyramus must draw a sword to kill himself, which the ladies cannot abide. How answer you that?

Snout. By'r lakin, a parlous[22] fear!

Starveling. I believe we must leave the killing out, when all is done.

---

18. **obscenely:** Bottom means "obscurely" or "off the scene."
19. **pat:** right on time.
20. **hawthorne brake:** thicket of hawthorn bushes.
21. **tiring-house:** dressing room.
22. **parlous:** perilous.

Bottom. Not a whit. I have a device to make all well. Write me a prologue, and let the prologue seem to say we will do no harm with our swords, and that Pyramus is not killed indeed. And, for the more better assurance, tell them that I Pyramus am not Pyramus, but Bottom, the weaver. This will put them out of fear.

Quince. Well, we will have such a prologue, and it shall be written in eight and six.[23]

Bottom. No, make it two more. Let it be written in eight and eight.

Snout. Will not the ladies be afeard of the lion?

Starveling. I fear it, I promise you.

Bottom. Masters, you ought to consider with yourselves. To bring in—God shield us—a lion among ladies is a most dreadful thing; for there is not a more fearful wild-fowl than your lion living, and we ought to look to 't.

Snout. Therefore another prologue must tell he is not a lion.

Bottom. Nay, you must name his name, and half his face must be seen through the lion's neck. And he himself must speak through, saying thus, or to the same defect[24]—"Ladies"—or "Fair ladies—I would wish you"—or "I would request you"—or "I would entreat you—not to fear, not to tremble. My life for yours. If you think I come hither as a lion, it were pity of my life. No, I am no such thing. I am a man as other men are." And there indeed let him name his name, and tell them plainly he is Snug the joiner.

Quince. Well, it shall be so. But there is two hard things: that is, to bring the moonlight into a chamber, for, you know, Pyramus and Thisby meet by moonlight.

---

23. **eight and six:** Ballads were commonly written in alternate lines of eight and six syllables.

24. **defect:** Bottom means "effect."

Snout. Doth the moon shine that night we play our play?

Bottom. A calendar, a calendar! Look in the almanac, find out moonshine, find out moonshine!

Quince. Yes, it doth shine that night.

Bottom. Why, then may you leave a casement of the great-chamber[25] window, where we play, open, and the moon may shine in at the casement.

Quince. Aye, or else one must come in with a bush of thorns and a lantern,[26] and say he comes to disfigure,[27] or to present, the person of moonshine. Then, there is another thing. We must have a wall in the great chamber, for Pyramus and Thisby, says the story, did talk through the chink of a wall.

Snout. You can never bring in a wall. What say you, Bottom?

Bottom. Some man or other must present wall. And let him have some plaster, or some loam, or some rough-cast[28] about him, to signify wall. And let him hold his fingers thus, and through that cranny shall Pyramus and Thisby whisper.

Quince. If that may be, then all is well. Come, sit down, every mother's son, and rehearse your parts. Pyramus, you begin. When you have spoken your speech, enter into that brake. And so everyone according to his cue. Speak, Pyramus. Thisby, stand forth.

Bottom (*as* **Pyramus**). "Thisby, the flowers of odious savors sweet—"

Quince. Odors, odors.

Bottom (*as* **Pyramus**). "—odors savors sweet. So hath thy breath, my dearest Thisby dear.

---

25. **great-chamber:** hall of a great house.
26. **bush . . . lantern:** supposedly carried by the man in the moon.
27. **disfigure:** Quince means "figure" or "portray."
28. **roughcast:** rough plaster.

But hark, a voice! Stay thou but here awhile,
And by and by I will to thee appear."

[*Exit.*]

Flute. Must I speak now?

Quince. Aye, marry must you, for you must understand he goes but to see a noise that he heard, and is to come again.

Flute (*as* **Thisby**). "Most radiant Pyramus, most lily-white of hue,

Of color like the red rose on triumphant brier,

Most briskly juvenal,[29] and eke[30] most lovely too,

As true as truest horse, that yet would never tire,

I'll meet thee, Pyramus, at Ninny's tomb."

Quince. "Ninus' tomb," man. Why, you must not speak that yet. That you answer to Pyramus. You speak all your part at once, cues and all. Pyramus enter. Your cue is past. It is "never tire."

Flute (*as* **Thisby**). Oh—

"As true as truest horse, that yet would never tire."

[*Reenter* BOTTOM.]

Bottom (*as* **Pyramus**). "If I were fair, Thisby, I were only thine."

[*At this point the rehearsal is broken up and the players scatter. They next meet to perform their play before the* DUKE *and his court.*]

---

29. **juvenal:** youthful.
30. **eke:** also.

Scene 3

Athens. The palace of THESEUS. *Enter* THESEUS, HIPPOLYTA, PHILOSTRATE, LORDS, *and* ATTENDANTS.

Theseus. Where is our usual manager of mirth? What
    revels are in hand? Is there no play? Call Philostrate.
Philostrate. Here, mighty Theseus.
Theseus. Say, what abridgment[31] have you for this
    evening?
    What masque?[32] What music? How shall we beguile
    The lazy time, if not with some delight?
Philostrate. A play there is, my lord, some ten words
    long,
    Which is as brief as I have known a play.
    But by ten words, my lord, it is too long,
    Which makes it tedious; for in all the play
    There is not one word apt, one player fitted.
    And tragical, my noble lord, it is,
    For Pyramus therein doth kill himself.
    Which, when I saw rehearsed, I must confess,
    Made mine eyes water, but more merry tears
    The passion of loud laughter never shed.
Theseus. What are they that do play it?
Philostrate. Hard-handed men that work in Athens here,
    Which never labored in their minds till now.
    And now have toiled their unbreathed[33] memories
    With this same play, against[34] your nuptial.
Theseus. I will hear that play,
    For never anything can be amiss,

---

31. **abridgment:** entertainment (to abridge, or shorten, the evening).
32. **masque:** court entertainment with masked actors.
33. **unbreathed:** unpracticed; inexperienced.
34. **against:** in anticipation of.

When simpleness and duty tender it.
Go, bring them in, and take your places, ladies.

[*As* PHILOSTRATE *leaves to get the players,* THESEUS *and the others arrange themselves on the side of the stage as an audience.* PHILOSTRATE *reenters.*]

Philostrate. So please your Grace, the Prologue is addressed.[35]

[*Flourish of trumpets. Enter* QUINCE *for the* Prologue.]

Quince (*as* **Prologue**). If[36] we offend, it is with our good will.
That you should think, we come not to offend,
But with good will. To show our simple skill,
That is the true beginning of our end.
Consider, then, we come but in despite.[37]
We do not come, as minding to content you,
Our true intent is. All for your delight,
We are not here. That you should here repent you,
The actors are at hand, and, by their show,
You shall know all, that you are like to know.
Theseus. This fellow does not stand upon points.[38]
First Courtier. He hath rid[39] his prologue like a rough colt, he knows not the stop. A good moral, my lord. It is not enough to speak, but to speak true.
Hippolyta. Indeed he hath played on his prologue like a child on a recorder—a sound, but not in government.[40]
Theseus. His speech was like a tangled chain—nothing impaired, but all disordered. Who is next?

---

35. **addressed:** ready.
36. **If . . . :** Because the prologue is mispunctuated, the meaning of Quince's speech is comically distorted.
37. **despite:** ill will.
38. **stand upon points:** pay attention to punctuation marks.
39. **rid:** ridden.
40. **not in government:** undisciplined.

[*Enter* PYRAMUS *and* THISBY, WALL, MOONSHINE, *and* LION.]

Quince (*as* **Prologue**). Gentles, perchance you wonder at this show,
But wonder on, till truth makes all things plain.
This man is Pyramus, if you would know.
This beauteous lady, Thisby is certain.
This man, with lime and roughcast, doth present
Wall, that vile Wall which did these lovers sunder,[41]
And through Wall's chink, poor souls, they are content
To whisper. At the which let no man wonder.
This man, with lantern, dog, and bush of thorn,
Presenteth Moonshine; for, if you will know,
By moonshine did these lovers think no scorn
To meet at Ninus' tomb, there, there to woo.
This grisly beast, which Lion hight[42] by name,
The trusty Thisby, coming first by night,
Did scare away, or rather did affright.
And, as she fled, her mantle she did fall,
Which Lion vile with bloody mouth did stain.
Anon comes Pyramus, sweet youth and tall,
And finds his trusty Thisby's mantle slain.
Whereat, with blade, with bloody blameful blade,
He bravely broached[43] his boiling bloody breast.
And Thisby, tarrying in mulberry shade,
His dagger drew, and died. For all the rest,
Let Lion, Moonshine, Wall, and lovers twain
At large[44] discourse, while here they do remain.

[*Exeunt* Prologue, PYRAMUS, THISBY, LION, *and* MOONSHINE.]

Theseus. I wonder if the lion be to speak.

---

41. **sunder:** separate.
42. **hight:** is called.
43. **broached:** stabbed.
44. **at large:** in full.

Second Courtier. No wonder, my Lord. One lion may, when many asses do.

Snout (*as* **Wall**). In this same interlude it doth befall
  That I, one Snout by name, present a wall,
  And such a wall, as I would have you think,
  That had in it a crannied hole or chink,
  Through which the lovers, Pyramus and Thisby,
  Did whisper often very secretly.
  This loam, this roughcast, and this stone doth show
  That I am that same wall. The truth is so.
  And this the cranny is, right and siníster,[45]
  Through which the fearful lovers are to whisper.

Theseus. Would you desire lime and hair to speak better?

Second Courtier. It is the wittiest partition that I ever heard discourse, my lord.

Theseus. Pyramus draws near the wall! Silence!

[*Reenter* PYRAMUS.]

Bottom (*as* **Pyramus**). O grim-looked night! O night with hue so black!
  O night, which ever art when day is not!
  O night, O night! alack, alack, alack,
  I fear my Thisby's promise is forgot!
  And thou, O wall, O sweet, O lovely wall,
  That stand'st between her father's ground and mine!
  Thou wall, O wall, O sweet and lovely wall,
  Show me thy chink, to blink through with mine eyne!

[WALL *holds up his fingers.*]

  Thanks, courteous wall. Jove shield thee well for this!
  But what see I? No Thisby do I see.
  O wicked wall, through whom I see no bliss!
  Cursed be thy stones for thus deceiving me!

---

45. **siníster:** left.

Theseus. The wall, methinks, being sensible,[46] should curse again.

Bottom. No, in truth, sir, he should not. "Deceiving me" is Thisby's cue. She is to enter now, and I am to spy her through the wall. You should see it will fall pat as I told you. Yonder she comes.

[*Reenter* THISBY.]

Flute (*as* **Thisby**). O wall, full often has thou heard my moans,

For parting my fair Pyramus and me!

My cherry lips have often kissed thy stones,

Thy stones with lime and hair knit up in thee.

Bottom (*as* **Pyramus**). I see a voice. Now will I to the chink,

To spy an I can hear my Thisby's face.

Thisby!

Flute (*as* **Thisby**). My love thou art, my love I think.

Bottom (*as* **Pyramus**). Think what thou wilt, I am thy lover's grace;

And like Limander,[47] am I trusty still.

Flute (*as* **Thisby**). And I, like Helen,[48] till the Fates[49] me kill.

Bottom (*as* **Pyramus**). Oh, kiss me through the hole of this vile wall!

Flute (*as* **Thisby**). I kiss the wall's hole, not your lips at all.

Bottom (*as* **Pyramus**). Wilt thou at Ninny's tomb meet me straightway?

---

46. **being sensible:** having feeling.
47. **Limander:** instead of *Leander,* a legendary Greek lover.
48. **Helen:** instead of *Hero,* Leander's love. Helen was in another legend.
49. **Fates:** In Greek mythology, the three goddesses who controlled the future.

Flute (*as* **Thisby**). 'Tide[50] life, 'tide death, I come without delay.

[*Exeunt* PYRAMUS *and* THISBY.]

Snout (*as* **Wall**). Thus have I, Wall, my part dischargèd so;
And, being done, thus Wall away doth go.   [*Exit* Wall.]

Theseus. Now is the mural[51] down between the two neighbors.

Second Courtier. No remedy, my lord, when walls are so willful to hear without warning.

Hippolyta. This is the silliest stuff that I ever heard.

Theseus. The best in this kind are but shadows, and the worst are no worse if imagination amend them.

Hippolyta. It must be your imagination then, and not theirs.

Theseus. If we imagine no worse of them than they of themselves, they may pass for excellent men. Here come two noble beasts in, a man and a lion.

[*Reenter* LION *and* MOONSHINE.]

Snug (*as* **Lion**). You, ladies, you, whose gentle hearts do fear
The smallest monstrous mouse that creeps on floor,
May now perchance[52] both quake and tremble here,
When lion rough in wildest rage doth roar.
Then know that I, one Snug, the joiner, am
A lion fell,[53] nor else no lion's dam;
For, if I should as lion come in strife
Into this place, 'twere pity on my life.[54]

---

50. **'tide:** betide; happen.
51. **mural:** wall.
52. **perchance:** perhaps.
53. **fell:** fierce. *Fell* also refers to an animal's hide or skin.
54. **'twere . . . life:** I should be hanged for it.

Theseus. A very gentle beast, and of a good conscience.

Second Courtier. The very best at a beast, my lord, that e'er I saw.

First Courtier. This lion is a very fox for his valor.

Starveling (*as* **Moonshine**). This lantern doth the hornèd moon present,

Myself the man i' the moon do seem to be.

Theseus. This is the greatest error of all the rest. The man should be put into the lantern. How is it else the man i' the moon?

First Courtier. Proceed, Moon.

Starveling. All that I have to say is, to tell you that the lantern is the moon; I, the man i' the moon; this thornbush, my thornbush; and this dog, my dog.

Second Courtier. Why, all these should be in the lantern, for all these are in the moon. But silence! Here comes Thisby.

[*Reenter* THISBY.]

Flute (*as* **Thisby**). This is old Ninny's tomb. Where is my love?

Snug (*as* **Lion,** *roaring*). Oh—   [Thisby *runs off.*]

Second Courtier. Well roared, Lion!

Theseus. Well run, Thisby!

Hippolyta. Well shone, Moon! Truly, the moon shines with a good grace.

[LION *shakes* THISBY's *mantle and exits.*]

Theseus. Well moused, Lion!

First Courtier. And so the lion vanished.

Second Courtier. And then came Pyramus.

[*Reenter* PYRAMUS.]

Bottom (*as* **Pyramus**). Sweet Moon, I thank thee for thy sunny beams,

I thank thee, Moon, for shining now so bright.
For, by thy gracious, golden, glittering gleams,
I trust to take of truest Thisby sight.
> But stay, oh spite!
> But mark, poor knight,
> What dreadful dole[55] is here!
> Eyes, do you see?
> How can it be?
> Oh dainty duck! Oh dear!
> Thy mantle good,
> What, stained with blood!
> Approach, ye Furies fell![56]
> O Fates, come, come,
> Cut thread and thrum[57]
> Quail, crush, conclude, and quell![58]

Theseus. This passion,[59] and the death of a dear friend,
would go near to make a man look sad.

Hippolyta. Beshrew my heart, but I pity the man.

Bottom (*as* **Pyramus**). O wherefore, Nature, didst thou
lions frame?
Since lion vile hath here deflowered my dear,
Which is—no, no—which was the fairest dame
That lived, that loved, that liked, that looked with
cheer.
> Come, tears, confound![60]
> Out, sword, and wound
> The pap[61] of Pyramus.

---

55. **dole:** sorrow.
56. **Furies fell:** In Greek mythology, the Furies avenged unpunished crimes.
57. **thrum:** the very end of the thread. One of the goddesses spun the thread
    of life, a second goddess determined its length, and a third cut it.
58. **quell:** slay.
59. **passion:** display of sorrow.
60. **confound:** destroy.
61. **pap:** breast.

Aye, that left pap,
Where heart doth hop.   *[Stabs himself.]*
Thus die I, thus, thus, thus.
Now am I dead,
Now am I fled,
My soul is in the sky.
Tongue, lose thy light,
Moon, take thy flight,   *[Exit* MOONSHINE.]
Now die, die, die, die, die.   *[Dies.]*

Theseus. With the help of a surgeon he might yet recover, and prove an ass.

Hippolyta. How chance Moonshine is gone before Thisby comes back and finds her lover?

Theseus. She will find him by starlight. Here she comes, and her passion ends the play.

[Reenter THISBY.]

Flute (*as* **Thisby**). Asleep, my love?
What, dead, my dove?
O Pyramus, arise!
Speak, speak. Quite dumb?
Dead, dead? A tomb
Must cover thy sweet eyes.
These lily lips,
This cherry nose,
These yellow cowslip cheeks,
Are gone, are gone.
Lovers, make moan.
His eyes were green as leeks.
O Sisters Three, [62]
Come, come to me,
With hands as pale as milk;
Lay them in gore,

---

62. **Sisters Three:** the Fates.

Since you have shore[63]
With shears his thread of silk.
Tongue, not a word.
Come, trusty sword,
Come, blade, my breast imbrue![64]   [*Stabs herself.*]
And, farewell, friends.
Thus Thisby ends.
Adieu, adieu, adieu!   [*Dies.*]

Theseus. Moonshine and Lion are left to bury the dead.

Second Courtier. Aye, and Wall too.

Bottom (*starting up*). No, I assure you; the wall is down that parted their fathers. Will it please you to see the epilogue?

Theseus. No epilogue, I pray you, for your play needs no excuse. Never excuse, for when the players are all dead, there need none to be blamed. Marry, if he that writ it had played Pyramus and hanged himself in Thisby's garter, it would have been a fine tragedy. And so it is, truly, and very notably discharged.

---

63. **shore:** shorn; cut.
64. **imbrue:** drench with blood.

William Shakespeare
(1564–1616)

The places where William Shakespeare began and ended his life are known. Millions of tourists from all over the world visit the house where he was born at Stratford-on-Avon and his tomb in the village church. However, many other details of Shakespeare's life remain a mystery. Since no one who actually knew Shakespeare ever wrote a biography of him, the only certain information we have about his life is in the form of public records and a few references to him made by his contemporaries.

In the sixteenth century, Stratford-on-Avon was a busy market town. Shakespeare's father, John, was a successful businessman and local politician who made and sold gloves. His mother, Mary Arden Shakespeare, came from an aristocratic Catholic family. Shakespeare was the third child, but the first one to survive infancy. A younger sister, Joan, lived to the age of seventy-seven and has descendants living today. All of William Shakespeare's direct descendants, his grandchildren, died young, without leaving children behind.

It seems likely that Shakespeare attended grammar school at Stratford, which provided an excellent elementary school education emphasizing the classics. When he was eighteen, he married Anne Hathaway, who was nine years older. Within three years of their marriage, they had three children: Susanna and twins Hamnet and Judith. Hamnet died at eleven, but the two daughters grew up and married.

When he was in his twenties, Shakespeare left Stratford and went to London to seek his fortune. There he joined an acting company. Because he had not gone to a university, as had many London writers, he probably worked his way up in the theater hierarchy, acting bit parts and revising plays for other dramatists before he began writing his own. He joined the Lord Chamberlain's Company, a group of actors and writers who produced plays and divided the profits. For this company he wrote thirty-seven plays, including tragedies, comedies, and histories, almost all brilliant and timeless.

The first London reference to Shakespeare comes in 1592, when Robert Greene, a popular, university-educated playwright of his time, wrote a pamphlet jealously attacking Shakespeare as "an upstart Crow, beautified with our feathers, that with his Tiger's heart wrapt in a players hide, supposes he is well able to bombast out a blank verse as the best of you. . . ." One of Greene's friends, Henry Chettle, immediately apologized in print to Shakespeare, defended his character, and commended his writing and acting ability.

At least in part because of the popular success of Shakespeare's plays, his company built the Globe, an outdoor theater outside London. It also owned Blackfriars, an indoor theater that produced Shakespeare's later plays.

In 1596, Shakespeare had his father apply to the Heralds College for a coat of arms, signifying that the family were "gentlefolks." The Shakespeare family crest displays a falcon shaking a spear. In 1597, Shakespeare began preparing for his retirement by buying a large estate at Stratford called New Place. Since he was by now part owner of both the Globe and Blackfriars, he was financially secure. Between 1610 and 1612, he moved back to Stratford. He wrote *The Tempest,* his last complete play, around 1611 and died five years later at the age of fifty-two.

Ben Jonson, a blunt, outspoken writer, knew Shakespeare well. In 1623, he published a poem declaring that Shakespeare, "star of poets," was superior to all Greek, Roman, and other English dramatists. Jonson was the first critic to make the prediction confirmed in every century, including our twenty-first, that Shakespeare would be "not of an age, but for all time."

The Elephant's Child

Rudyard Kipling
dramatized by Mara Rockliff

Characters

Narrator
The Elephant's Child
Kolokolo Bird
A Bi-Colored-Python-Rock-Snake
A Crocodile

Setting: Africa

All the characters are onstage. (They sit quietly until their turn comes to act out their parts.) The NARRATOR *steps forward and begins.*

Narrator. In the high and far-off times the elephant had no trunk. He had only a blackish, bulgy nose, as big as a boot, that he could wriggle about from side to side—but he couldn't pick up things with it. But there was one elephant—a new elephant—an Elephant's Child—

Elephant. That's me!

Narrator. The Elephant's Child was full of 'satiable curiosity, and that meant he asked ever so many questions.

Elephant. Who, me?

Narrator. He lived in Africa, and he filled all Africa with his 'satiable curiosity.

Elephant. Aunt Ostrich, why do your tail feathers grow just so?

Narrator. And his tall aunt, the ostrich, spanked him with her hard, hard claw.

Elephant. Ow! (*pause*) Uncle Giraffe, what makes your skin spotty?

Narrator. And his tall uncle, the giraffe, spanked him with his hard, hard hoof.

Elephant. Ow!

Narrator. And still he was full of 'satiable curiosity!

Elephant. Aunt Hippopotamus, why are your eyes red?

Narrator. And his broad aunt, the hippopotamus, spanked him with her broad, broad hoof.

Elephant. Ow! (*pause*) Uncle Baboon, why do melons taste just so?

Narrator. And his hairy uncle, the baboon, spanked him with his hairy, hairy paw.

Elephant. Ow!

Narrator. And *still* he was full of 'satiable curiosity! He asked questions about everything that he saw, or heard, or felt, or smelt, or touched, and all his uncles and his aunts spanked him.

Elephant. Ow! Ow! Ow!

Narrator. And still he was full of 'satiable curiosity! (*pause*) One fine morning this 'satiable Elephant's Child asked a new fine question that he had never asked before.

Elephant. What does the Crocodile have for dinner?

Narrator. Then everybody said, "Hush!" in a loud and dretful tone, and they spanked him immediately and directly, without stopping, for a long time.

Elephant. Ow!

Narrator. By and by, when that was finished, he came upon Kolokolo Bird—

Bird. That's me!

Narrator. —sitting in the middle of a wait-a-bit thorn bush.

Elephant. Kolokolo Bird, my father has spanked me, and my mother has spanked me, and all my aunts and uncles have spanked me for my 'satiable curiosity. And *still* I want to know what the Crocodile has for dinner!

Bird (*in a mournful cry*). Go to the banks of the great gray-green greasy Limpopo River, all set about with fever-trees, and find out.

Narrator. That very next morning, this 'satiable Elephant's Child took a hundred pounds of bananas—the little short red kind—and a hundred pounds of sugar cane—the long purple kind—and seventeen melons—the greeny-crackly kind—and said goodbye to all his dear families.

Elephant. Goodbye. I am going to the great gray-green greasy Limpopo River, all set about with fever-trees, to find out what the Crocodile has for dinner.

Narrator. And they all spanked him once more for luck, though he asked them most politely to stop.

Elephant. Ow! Please stop.

Narrator. Then he went away, eating melons, and throwing the rind about, because he had no trunk to pick it up. He went east by north, eating melons all the time, till at last he came to the banks of the great gray-green greasy Limpopo River, all set about with fever-trees, precisely as Kolokolo Bird had said.

Elephant. It sure is greasy.

Narrator. The first thing that he found was a Bi-Colored-Python-Rock-Snake curled round a rock.

Snake. That's me!

Elephant (*politely*). Excuse me, but have you seen such a thing as a Crocodile in these parts?

Narrator. Now you must know and understand that till that very week, and day, and hour, and minute, this 'satiable Elephant's Child had never seen a Crocodile, and did not know what one was like. It was all his 'satiable curiosity.

Snake (*with deep scorn*). *Have* I seen a crocodile? What will you ask me next?

Elephant (*politely*). 'Scuse me, but could you kindly tell me what he has for dinner?

Narrator. Then the Bi-Colored-Python-Rock-Snake uncoiled himself very quickly from the rock and spanked the Elephant's Child with his scalesome, flailsome tail.

Elephant. Ow! (*pause*) My father and my mother and my uncle and my aunt, not to mention my other aunt, the hippopotamus, and my other uncle, the baboon, have all spanked me for my 'satiable curiosity—and I suppose this is the same thing.

Narrator. So he said goodbye very politely to the Bi-Colored-Python-Rock-Snake—

Elephant (*politely*). Goodbye, Bi-Colored-Python-Rock-Snake.

Narrator. —and helped to coil him up on the rock again, and went on, eating melons and throwing the rind about because he could not pick it up, till he trod on what he thought was a log of wood at the very edge of the great gray-green greasy Limpopo River, all set about with fever-trees. But it was really the Crocodile—

Crocodile. That's me!

Narrator. —and the Crocodile winked one eye—like this!

[*The* NARRATOR *and the* CROCODILE *both wink in an exaggerated way.*]

Elephant (*politely*). 'Scuse me, but do you happen to have seen a crocodile in these parts?

Narrator. Then the Crocodile winked the other eye, and lifted half his tail out of the mud. And the Elephant's Child stepped back most politely, because he did not wish to be spanked again.

Crocodile. Come hither, little one. Why do you ask such things?

Elephant (*politely*). 'Scuse me, but my father has spanked me, my mother has spanked me, not to mention my tall aunt, the ostrich, and my tall uncle, the giraffe, who can kick ever so hard, as well as my broad aunt, the hippopotamus, and my hairy uncle, the baboon, *and* including the Bi-Colored-Python-Rock-Snake, with the scalesome, flailsome tail, just up the bank, who spanks harder than any of them. And *so,* if it's quite all the same to you, I don't want to be spanked any more.

Crocodile. Come hither, little one, for I am the Crocodile.

Narrator. And he wept crocodile tears to show it was quite true.

Elephant. You are the very person I have been looking for all these long days. Will you please tell me what you have for dinner?

Crocodile. Come hither, little one, and I'll whisper.

[*The characters begin to pantomime the action as the* NARRATOR *describes it.*]

Narrator. Then the Elephant's Child put his head down close to the Crocodile's musky, tusky mouth, and the Crocodile caught him by his little nose, which up to that very week, day, hour, and minute had been no bigger than a boot, though much more useful.

Crocodile (*through his teeth*). I think—I think today I will begin with Elephant's Child!

Elephant (*through his nose*). Led go! You are hurtig be!

Narrator. Then the Bi-Colored-Python-Rock-Snake scuffled down from the bank and said—

Snake. My young friend, if you do not now, immediately and instantly, pull as hard as ever you can, it is my opinion that your acquaintance in the large-pattern leather overcoat—

Crocodile. That's me!

Snake. —will jerk you into yonder limpid stream before you can say Jack Robinson.

Narrator. This is the way Bi-Colored-Python-Rock-Snakes always talk. (*pause*) Then the Elephant's Child sat back and pulled, and pulled, and pulled, and his nose began to stretch. And the Crocodile floundered into the water, making it all creamy with great sweeps of his tail, and *he* pulled, and pulled, and pulled. And the Elephant's Child's nose kept on stretching. And the Elephant's Child planted his four little legs and pulled, and pulled, and pulled, and his nose kept on stretching. And the Crocodile threshed his tail like an oar, and *he* pulled, and pulled, and pulled, and at each pull the Elephant's Child's nose grew longer and longer—and it hurt him hijjus!

Elephant. Ow!

Narrator. Then the Elephant's Child felt his legs slipping, and he said through his nose, which was now nearly five feet long—

Elephant. This is too butch for be!

Narrator. Then the Bi-Colored-Python-Rock-Snake came down from the bank and knotted himself in a double clove hitch round the Elephant's Child's hind legs.

Snake. Rash and inexperienced traveler, we will now seriously devote ourselves to a little high tension, because if we do not, it is my impression that yonder self-propelling man-of-war with the armor-plated upper deck—

Crocodile. That's me!

Snake.—will permanently vitiate your future career!

Narrator. That is the way all Bi-Colored-Python-Rock-Snakes always talk. (*pause*) So he pulled, and the Elephant's Child pulled, and the Crocodile pulled. But the Elephant's Child and the Bi-Colored-Python-Rock-Snake pulled hardest. And at last the Crocodile let go of the Elephant's Child's nose with a plop that you could hear all up and down the Limpopo.

[*The* ELEPHANT'S CHILD *falls back on the* SNAKE, *then gets up and helps him up.*]

Elephant. Thank you, Bi-Colored-Python-Rock-Snake!
Narrator. Next he was kind to his poor pulled nose, and wrapped it all up in cool banana leaves, and hung it in the great gray-green greasy Limpopo to cool.
Snake. What are you doing that for?
Elephant. 'Scuse me, but my nose is badly out of shape and I am waiting for it to shrink.
Snake. Then you will have to wait a long time. Some people do not know what is good for them.
Narrator. The Elephant's Child sat there for three days waiting for his nose to shrink. But it never grew any shorter. For you will see and understand that the Crocodile had pulled it out into a really truly trunk same as all elephants have today. (*pause*) At the end of the third day a fly came and stung him on the shoulder—
Elephant. Ow!
Narrator. —and before he knew what he was doing he lifted up his trunk and hit that fly dead with the end of it.
Snake. 'Vantage number one! You couldn't have done that with a mere-smear nose. Try and eat a little now.
Narrator. Before he thought what he was doing the Elephant's Child put out his trunk and plucked a large bundle of grass, dusted it clean against his forelegs, and stuffed it into his own mouth.
Snake. 'Vantage number two! You couldn't have done that with a mere-smear nose. Don't you think the sun is very hot here?

Elephant. It is.

Narrator. And before he thought what he was doing he schlooped up a schloop of mud from the banks of the great gray-green greasy Limpopo, and slapped it on his head, where it made a cool schloopy-sloshy mud-cap all trickly behind his ears.

Snake. 'Vantage number three! You couldn't have done that with a mere-smear nose. Now, how do you feel about being spanked again?

Elephant (*politely*). 'Scuse me, but I should not like it at all.

Snake. How would you like to spank somebody?

Elephant. I should like it very much indeed.

Snake. Well, you will find that new nose of yours very useful to spank people with.

Elephant. Thank you. I'll remember that. And now I think I'll go home to all my dear family and try.

Narrator. So the Elephant's Child went home across Africa frisking and whisking his trunk. When he wanted fruit to eat he pulled fruit down from a tree, instead of waiting for it to fall as he used to. When he wanted grass he plucked grass up from the ground, instead of going on his knees as he used to. When the flies bit him he broke off the branch of a tree and used it as a fly whisk, and he made himself a new, cool, slushy-squshy mud-cap whenever the sun was hot. When he felt lonely walking through Africa he sang to himself down his trunk, and the noise was louder than several brass bands. The rest of the time he picked up the melon rinds that he had dropped on his way to the Limpopo, for he was a tidy pachyderm. (*pause*) One dark evening he came back to all his dear families. He coiled up his trunk and said—

Elephant. How do you do?

[*The* BIRD, SNAKE, *and* CROCODILE *pretend to be the* ELEPHANT'S CHILD's *family.*]

Narrator. They were very glad to see him and immediately said—

Bird. Come here and be spanked for your 'satiable curiosity.

Elephant. Pooh. I don't think you peoples know anything about spanking. But *I* do, and I'll show you.

Narrator. Then he uncurled his trunk and knocked two of his dear brothers head over heels.

Snake. Oh bananas! Where did you learn that trick, and what have you done to your nose?

Elephant. I got a new one from the Crocodile on the banks of the great gray-green greasy Limpopo River. I asked him what he had for dinner, and he gave me this to keep.

Crocodile. It looks very ugly.

Elephant. It does. But it's very useful.

Narrator. And he picked up his hairy uncle, the baboon, by one hairy leg, and hove him into a hornets' nest. Then that bad Elephant's Child spanked all his dear families for a long time.

Bird. Ow!

Snake. Ow!

Crocodile. Ow! Ow! Ow!

Narrator. At last things grew so exciting that his dear families went off one by one in a hurry to the banks of the great gray-green greasy Limpopo River, all set about with fever-trees, to borrow new noses from the Crocodile. When they came back nobody spanked anybody anymore. And ever since that day, all the elephants you will ever see, besides all those that you won't, have trunks precisely like the trunk of the 'satiable Elephant's Child.

Elephant. That's me!

Rudyard Kipling
(1865–1936)

India was the country that Rudyard Kipling first called home, and Hindi, spoken by his Indian nursemaid, was his first language. As a child, whenever he was taken to spend time with his parents, the servants had to remind him to speak English. Kipling's parents moved to India on the day they were married, the year before Rudyard was born in Bombay.

Kipling's mother was a charming, talented woman, the oldest daughter in the large family of a well-known but poorly paid minister. Kipling's father, also the son of a minister, became a teacher of industrial art at the School of Art in Bombay.

An event that changed Kipling's life occurred when he was still a young child. Most Anglo-Indians (English subjects living in India) sent their children to England to be educated, but six-year-old Rudyard and his three-year-old sister were unusually young when their parents shipped them back to England. There were many wealthy relatives who might have kept the children, but Kipling's mother was a proud woman who did not want to depend on relatives. Without any explanation from their parents, Kipling and his sister were left with strangers in a place that he later called the "House of Desolation." For the next five years, Kipling's foster parents, who considered him a spoiled and naughty child, regularly starved and beat him. Like the Elephant's Child, Kipling asked too many questions they could not answer.

At the age of twelve, Kipling was sent to a cheap boarding school, where he continued to have a rough time. His eyesight was so poor that he could not participate in sports, which were even more important in that time and place than they are today. Instead, he spent a great deal of time reading, and he began to write poetry.

Because his parents could not afford to send Kipling to a university, he returned to India when he was sixteen and took a job as an editor for an English-language newspaper. He lived with his parents, whom he loved and admired despite those lonely years in England. He worked hard, even running the newspaper office for several months. The lives of British colonials, in a society built on official rank, fascinated him. Kipling contrasted their attitudes and customs with those of the Indian people they ruled.

Soon the paper was printing Kipling's light verse and short stories. Collected in inexpensive editions and distributed in England, these books, with their exotic settings, characters, and themes, seemed magically new. Nothing like them had been written before. His recurrent themes were the difference between East and West and the value of each culture. Readers clamored for more. By the time he returned to England at the age of twenty-four, Kipling was already famous. He eventually became the most popular prose writer since Charles Dickens, and he was acclaimed by critics as diverse as Oscar Wilde and Henry James.

Kipling married an American and lived in Vermont for several years. He wrote *The Jungle Book* and *Captains Courageous* there. After the death of their older daughter, the Kiplings returned to England. Over the next half century, Kipling wrote dozens of books, and in 1907, he became the first British writer to win the Nobel Prize in literature.

A Mad Tea Party

From *Alice's Adventures in Wonderland*

Lewis Carroll
dramatized by Mara Rockliff

Characters
The March Hare
The Hatter
The Dormouse
Alice

Setting: Wonderland

There is a large table covered in a tablecloth, with many places set for tea. (A cup and saucer and teaspoon at each place; a teapot and a platter of bread and butter in the middle.) The MARCH HARE, *the* HATTER, *and the* DORMOUSE *are all crowded at one end of the table. The* DORMOUSE *is sleeping between the other two, who are using it as a cushion, resting their elbows on it and talking over its head. As* ALICE *approaches, the* MARCH HARE *and the* HATTER *shout, "No room! No room!"*

Alice (*indignantly*). There's *plenty* of room!

[*She sits at the table. The* HATTER *watches her with great curiosity.*]

March Hare (*encouragingly*). Have some wine.

[*Alice looks around the table.*]

Alice. I don't see any wine.
March Hare. There isn't any.

Alice (*angrily*). Then it wasn't very civil of you to offer it.
March Hare. It wasn't very civil of you to sit down without being invited.
Alice. I didn't know it was *your* table. It's laid for a great many more than three.
Hatter (*to* ALICE). Your hair wants cutting.
Alice. You should learn not to make personal remarks. It's very rude.

[*The* HATTER *opens his eyes wide.*]

Hatter. Why is a raven like a writing desk?
Alice (*to herself*). We'll have some fun now! I'm glad they've begun asking riddles. (*to the group*) I believe I can guess that.
March Hare. Do you mean that you think you can find out the answer to it?
Alice. Exactly so.
March Hare. Then you should say what you mean.
Alice. I do! At least—at least I mean what I say—that's the same thing, you know.
Hatter. Not the same thing a bit! Why, you might just as well say that "I see what I eat" is the same thing as "I eat what I see"!
March Hare. You might just as well say that "I like what I get" is the same thing as "I get what I like"!

[*The* DORMOUSE *raises its head.*]

Dormouse (*sleepily*). You might just as well say that "I breathe when I sleep" is the same thing as "I sleep when I breathe"!
Hatter. It *is* the same thing with you.

[*They are all silent for a moment. The* DORMOUSE *falls asleep again. The* HATTER *takes out a large, old-fashioned pocket watch on a chain. He looks at it uneasily, then shakes it and holds it up to his ear.*]

Hatter (*to* ALICE). What day of the month is it?

[ALICE *thinks.*]

Alice. The fourth.

Hatter. Two days wrong! (*to the* MARCH HARE, *angrily*) I told you butter wouldn't suit the works!

March Hare (*meekly*). It was the *best* butter.

Hatter (*grumbling*). Yes, but some crumbs must have gotten in as well. You shouldn't have put it in with the bread knife.

[*The* MARCH HARE *takes the watch and looks at it gloomily, then dips it into his cup of tea and looks at it again.* ALICE *gets up and looks over his shoulder.*]

March Hare. It was the *best* butter, you know.

Alice. What a funny watch! It tells the day of the month, and doesn't tell what o'clock it is!

Hatter. Why should it? Does *your* watch tell you what year it is?

Alice. Of course not. But that's because it stays the same year for such a long time together.

Hatter. Which is just the case with *mine*.

[ALICE *looks puzzled.*]

Alice (*politely*). I don't quite understand you.

[*She sits down again.*]

Hatter. The Dormouse is asleep again.

[*The* HATTER *pours a little tea on the* DORMOUSE's *nose. The* DORMOUSE *shakes its head impatiently but does not open its eyes.*]

Dormouse. Of course, of course. Just what I was going to remark myself.

Hatter (*to* ALICE). Have you guessed the riddle yet?

Alice. No, I give it up. What's the answer?

Hatter. I haven't the slightest idea.

March Hare. Nor I.

[ALICE *sighs wearily.*]

Alice. I think you might do something better with the time than wasting it in asking riddles that have no answers.

Hatter. If you knew Time as well as I do, you wouldn't talk about wasting *it*. It's *him*.

Alice. I don't know what you mean.

[*The* HATTER *tosses his head contemptuously.*]

Hatter. Of course you don't! I dare say you never even spoke to Time!

Alice (*cautiously*). Perhaps not, but I know I have to beat time when I learn music.

Hatter. Ah! That accounts for it. He won't stand beating. Now, if you only kept on good terms with him, he'd do almost anything you liked with the clock. For instance, suppose it were nine o'clock in the morning, just time to begin lessons. You'd only have to whisper a hint to Time, and round goes the clock in a twinkling! Half past one, time for dinner!

March Hare (*to itself*). I only wish it was.

Alice (*to the* HATTER, *thoughtfully*). That would be grand, certainly, but then—I shouldn't be hungry for it, you know.

Hatter. Not at first, perhaps, but you could keep it to half past one as long as you liked.

Alice. Is that the way *you* manage?

[*The* HATTER *shakes his head mournfully.*]

Hatter. Not I! We quarreled last March—just before he (*points with his teaspoon at the* MARCH HARE) went mad, you know. It was at the great concert given by the Queen of Hearts, and I had to sing (*sings to the tune of* "*Twinkle, Twinkle, Little Star*") "Twinkle, twinkle, little bat! How I wonder what you're at!" You know the song, perhaps?

Alice. I've heard something like it.

Hatter. It goes on, you know, in this way: (*sings*) "Up above the world you fly, like a tea tray in the sky. Twinkle, twinkle—"

[*The* DORMOUSE *shakes itself and begins singing in its sleep, interrupting the* HATTER.]

Dormouse. "Twinkle, twinkle, twinkle, twinkle, twinkle, twinkle, twinkle—"

[*The* HATTER *and the* MARCH HARE *pinch the* DORMOUSE *and it stops singing.*]

Hatter. Well, I'd hardly finished the first verse when the Queen bawled out, "He's murdering the time! Off with his head!"

Alice. How dreadfully savage!

Hatter (*mournfully*). And ever since that, he won't do a thing I ask! It's always six o'clock now.

[ALICE *gets an idea.*]

Alice. Is that the reason so many tea things are put out here?

[*The* HATTER *sighs.*]

Hatter. Yes, that's it. It's always tea time, and we've no time to wash the things between whiles.

Alice. Then you keep moving round, I suppose?

[*She gestures in a circle around the table.*]

Hatter. Exactly so, as the things get used up.

Alice. But what happens when you come to the beginning again?

[*The* MARCH HARE *yawns.*]

March Hare. Suppose we change the subject. I'm getting tired of this. I vote the young lady tells us a story.

Alice (*alarmed*). I'm afraid I don't know one.

March Hare and **Hatter** (*in unison*). Then the Dormouse shall! Wake up, Dormouse!

[*They pinch the* DORMOUSE, *which slowly opens its eyes.*]

Dormouse (*in a hoarse, feeble voice*). I wasn't asleep. I heard every word you fellows were saying.

March Hare. Tell us a story!

Alice. Yes, please do!

Hatter. And be quick about it, or you'll be asleep again before it's done.

Dormouse (*hurriedly*). Once upon a time there were three little sisters and their names were Elsie, Lacie, and Tillie; and they lived at the bottom of a well—

Alice. What did they live on?

[*The* DORMOUSE *thinks for a moment.*]

Dormouse. They lived on treacle.

Alice (*gently*). They couldn't have done that, you know. They'd have been ill.

Dormouse. So they were. *Very* ill.

[ALICE *looks puzzled.*]

Alice. But why did they live at the bottom of a well?

March Hare (*to* ALICE, *earnestly*). Take some more tea.

Alice (*offended*). I've had nothing yet, so I can't take more.

Hatter. You mean you can't take *less*. It's very easy to take *more* than nothing.

Alice. Nobody asked *your* opinion.

Hatter (*triumphantly*). Who's making personal remarks now?

[ALICE *has no reply. She takes some tea and bread and butter, then turns to the* DORMOUSE *again.*]

Alice (*to the* DORMOUSE). Why did they live at the bottom of a well?

[*The* DORMOUSE *thinks again.*]

Dormouse. It was a treacle well.

Alice (*angrily*). There's no such thing!

[*The* HATTER *and the* MARCH HARE *shush her.*]

Dormouse (*sulkily*). If you can't be civil, you'd better finish the story for yourself.

Alice (*humbly*). No, please go on! I won't interrupt you again. I dare say there may be *one*.

Dormouse (*indignantly*). One, indeed! And so these three little sisters—they were learning to draw, you know—

Alice. What did they draw?

Dormouse. Treacle.

Hatter. I want a clean cup. Let's all move one place on.

[*Everyone moves one place to the right.*]

Alice (*to the* DORMOUSE, *cautiously*). But I don't understand. Where did they draw the treacle from?

Hatter. You can draw water out of a water well, so I should think you could draw treacle out of a treacle well—eh, stupid?

[ALICE *ignores the* HATTER *and speaks to the* DORMOUSE.]

Alice. But they were *in* the well.
Dormouse. Of course they were. Well in.

[ALICE *falls silent, confused. The* DORMOUSE *resumes its story sleepily, yawning and rubbing its eyes.*]

Dormouse. They were learning to draw, and they drew all manner of things—everything that begins with an *M*—
Alice. Why with an *M*?
March Hare. Why not?

[*The* DORMOUSE *has closed its eyes and nodded off. The* HATTER *pinches the* DORMOUSE, *who wakes up with a little shriek and continues.*]

Dormouse. —That begins with an *M*, such as mouse traps, and the moon, and memory, and muchness—you know, you say things are "much of a muchness"—did you ever see such a thing as a drawing of a muchness?
Alice (*confused*). Really, now you ask me, I don't think—
Hatter. Then you shouldn't talk.

[ALICE *gets up in disgust and walks off. The* DORMOUSE *falls asleep immediately. The* HATTER *and the* MARCH HARE *begin trying to put the* DORMOUSE *into the teapot.* ALICE *looks back twice, but nobody notices she has left.*]

Alice. At any rate I'll never go *there* again! It's the stupidest tea party I ever was at in all my life!

[*She exits.*]

Lewis Carroll
(1832–1898)

The teacher of mathematics at Oxford University and clergyman in the Church of England was Reverend Charles Lutwidge Dodgson. The writer of *Alice's Adventures in Wonderland* and its sequel, *Through the Looking Glass*, was Lewis Carroll. Both were two halves of one fascinating, eccentric, and brilliant personality who sometimes signed his letters *Charles L. Dodgson,* sometimes signed them *Lewis Carroll,* his pen name, and sometimes even signed both names.

Dodgson's father was a devout and hard-working clergyman, who supplemented his small income by teaching. His mother was described as a gentle and patient woman of deep religious faith who had an unusually close and loving bond with Charles, her oldest son. There were eleven children; Charles had seven sisters, two older and five younger. He also had three younger brothers. As a child, he was always in charge of family entertainment, inventing and performing magic tricks, puppet plays, and ingenious games. He kept notebooks of sketches, poems, and stories that he created for the other children's enjoyment.

Dodgson was educated at home until he was twelve, then sent to boarding school, which he disliked intensely. He won prizes for his scholarship, but the other boys teased him because he preferred reading to sports. He also stammered when he was nervous, a condition that bothered him all of his life.

Two days after he started his college career, at Oxford University, Dodgson's mother died unexpectedly, possibly from typhoid or cholera. Her loss devastated Dodgson and left him with a fear of infection. As an undergraduate at Christ Church, one of the colleges at Oxford University, he received a kind of scholarship grant that provided him with an income for the rest of his life. Two conditions of the grant were that he remain unmarried and that he take holy orders, which would qualify him to become a priest in the Church of England. His stammer made preaching difficult, but it disappeared when he was around children, who loved to hear the stories he told.

Dodgson spent at least half of his days in the quiet, serious academic environment, but he also spent many sunlit days in the company of children, writing nonsense verse, creating puzzles, and pursuing his hobby of photography. Once Dodgson went on a picnic with the three young Liddell sisters, one of whom was named Alice. He told them a story he had made up about a girl named Alice who went down a rabbit hole into a fabulous wonderland. The real Alice made Dodgson promise to write down the story for her when he got home, which he did. That was the beginning of *Alice's Adventures in Wonderland*, from which the poem "Jabberwocky" is taken.

Modern linguists quote extensively from *Alice in Wonderland*, for the book's wild wordplay often illustrates serious linguistic principles. Unlike many books of that time, *Alice in Wonderland* is not at all sentimental. In fact, sentimentality is one of the targets of its satire.

Dodgson once claimed that mathematics is the true wonderland, "for nothing is impossible" there. Charles Dodgson was not an outstanding mathematician, but he did make original contributions to the study of formal logic.

Dodgson had many adult friends, but Lewis Carroll preferred the company of children. One of his young friends said, "He was one of us, and never a grown-up pretending to be a child in order to preach at us. . . ." Looking back at his life, Lewis Carroll wrote in 1896, "The friendship of children has always been a great element in my enjoyment of life, and is very *restful* as a contrast to the society of books, or of men."

The Legend of Sleepy Hollow

Washington Irving
dramatized by **Mara Rockliff**

Characters

Two travelers
An elderly innkeeper
Two schoolchildren
Ichabod Crane
Katrina Van Tassel
Brom Van Brunt
Katrina's mother
Katrina's father

Setting: Sleepy Hollow, a small village on the Hudson River in upstate New York.

Prologue

The village inn, 1819.

Two TRAVELERS *sit at a table.* TRAVELER 1 *leans back, stretches and yawns contentedly.* TRAVELER 2 *frowns and looks at his pocket watch.*

Traveler 1. Sleepy Hollow. What a perfect name for this quiet little valley. What a perfect place to spend the night. **Traveler 2** (*grumbling*). Sleepy Hollow. What a perfect place to spend the night waiting for our suppers. What a perfect name for the village with the slowest innkeeper in the world.

Traveler 1. Oh, but you know the food is always worth the wait. And he's sure to entertain us with a story while we eat.

Traveler 2 (*sarcastically*). Oh, yes, the stories. Which one do you think we'll hear this time? The absolutely true story of the time his wife's second cousin's brother-in-law saw the ghost of John André, the British spy who helped Benedict Arnold turn traitor?

Traveler 1. You know, they did capture him near here. You can still see the bridge where—

Traveler 2. Or perhaps the story his sister once heard from a man whose great-grandmother told him, of the Iroquois medicine man who cast a spell over this valley. Maybe that explains why the people here are so almighty slow and sleepy.

[*The* INNKEEPER *comes up from behind with their dinners on a tray, startling* TRAVELER 2.]

Innkeeper. Absolutely true! Long before Henry Hudson came exploring up the river, that was. Yup, plenty of unusual occurrences around these parts. I could tell you—

Traveler 2 (*to* TRAVELER 1). And I just bet he will, too.

Innkeeper. But I forget, you're travelin' folk. I guess you must have seen everything by now. Twice, maybe. You wouldn't think much of a little local peculiarity like a headless horseman.

Traveler 1. A headless horseman?

[*The* INNKEEPER *takes a seat at the table and pulls out a pipe.* TRAVELER 2 *groans.*]

Innkeeper. It's nothing much. Just a Hessian trooper got his head blown off by a cannonball. That was in the War for Independence, of course. Guess you're both too young to have fought. I was just a young fellow myself when I joined up. Now, I could tell you—

Traveler 1. But what about the headless horseman?

Innkeeper. Oh. Oh, yes. Well, they took him down to the churchyard and buried him—his body, anyway. Buried him good and deep. Seems he just couldn't rest easy without his head, though. Don't know what use he had for it, being dead and all.

Traveler 2 (*to* TRAVELER 1). Some of the living people around here don't seem to find much use for theirs, either.

Traveler 1 (*to* INNKEEPER). What happened?

Innkeeper. Well, seeing his head was missing, he went looking for it. Natural enough, I suppose.

Traveler 2 (*sarcastically*). If he had eyes somewhere below his neck, maybe.

Innkeeper (*oblivious*). Why, that very night the ghost of the German rider rose up out of the grave and galloped back to the battlefield, searching for his lost head.

Traveler 2. Lucky they buried him sitting on his horse. Otherwise he might have had to walk.

Traveler 1 (*to the* INNKEEPER). Did he find it?

Innkeeper. No, not that night nor any other night. But he's never stopped searching. In fact—listen!

[*They all fall silent for a moment.*]

Traveler 2. All I hear is the wind.

Traveler 1. And the rattle of tree branches against the window . . . I think.

Innkeeper. Not the faint, ghostly clatter of horse's hooves disappearing into the distance? Not the *whoosh* of a long black coat billowing out behind?

Traveler 2. All I hear is the wind. (*Under his breath*) Wind*bag.*

Innkeeper. Well, I hope you gentlemen sleep soundly tonight. I'm sure you'll find the accommodations to your liking. But if you should happen to be wakeful in the early hours, have a look out the window. Could be you'll glimpse the headless horseman charging by, anxious to return to his place in the churchyard before daybreak.

Traveler 1. What a story!

Traveler 2 (*sarcastically*). What a storyteller! And I suppose you will tell us it's all absolutely true.

Innkeeper. As to that, I couldn't say. Never seen him myself. But I'll tell you of someone who sure enough did, about thirty years back. Fellow from Connecticut. Came here to be our new village schoolmaster. Crane, his name was. Ichabod Crane . . .

Act One
In front of the village schoolhouse, 1790.

Two SCHOOLCHILDREN *run out of the schoolhouse, laughing. They turn and call back, hopping on one leg and flapping their arms like wings.*

Children. Crane, Crane, you old birdbrain! Schoolmaster Crane is an old birdbrain!

Child 1. But he sure doesn't *eat* like a bird, does he?

Child 2. I heard he ate half a baked ham all by himself, over at the Van Tassels' last Sunday after church. Three great big bowls of corn puddin', too.

Child 1. Guess all that psalm-singin' is hungry work. (*Whoops like a crane in imitation of* CRANE's *singing:*) Hoo, hoo, hoo!

[ICHABOD CRANE *rushes out, angrily waving a switch. In his other hand he carries a book. He is tall and thin, dressed shabbily in dark, ill-fitting clothing. The* CHILDREN *retreat to a safe distance.*]

Crane. Hans Van Brunt, you are asking for a whipping!

Child 1. You just try it! Lay a finger on me and my big brother Brom will pay you back double.

Child 2. Brom's been hoppin' mad ever since School-master Crane started courtin' Katrina Van Tassel. I heard him say if Crane didn't quit he'd fold him up and lay him on a shelf right in his own schoolhouse.

Crane. Brom Van Brunt is an ignorant lout. Who can blame Katrina if she prefers a man who appreciates the finer things in life? The intellectual, the spiritual—

Child 1 (*mocking*). The fine vitt-oo-als on her tabe-oo-al.

Child 2. Brom isn't a lout! He's bigger and stronger than any man in the whole valley. Best horseback rider for miles around, too. He's never lost a fight or a race. Everybody knows that.

Child 1. Crane's just sore 'cause Brom taught his dog to sing psalms better than he can. (*Whines and howls like a dog:*) Ow-ow-oooooooh!

[CRANE *advances on the* CHILDREN, *brandishing his switch. They run offstage.* CRANE *follows and almost bumps into* KATRINA VAN TASSEL *entering. His manner changes instantly from enraged to fawning. He sweeps a low bow.*]

Crane. Why, Miss Van Tassel. How perfectly delightful to see you. How extraordinarily charming you look today.

Katrina (*flirtatiously*). Oh, Mr. Crane, I'm sure I look just the same as always.

Crane. So true, Miss Van Tassel. Every day you look quite as extraordinarily charming as the day before, and every day I am astonished yet again by just how extraordinarily charming you invariably look.

Katrina. Oh, Mr. Crane. All your fancy talk is enough to turn a girl's head. You must get it out of that book you're always carrying around.

Crane. Ah, Miss Van Tassel. If only I might study such a happy subject as that of your matchless grace and elegance. But this book tells a darker tale, a grim and terrible tale of evil doings. It is a history of witchcraft in New England, written by the Reverend Cotton Mather.

Katrina. Oh, Mr. Crane! How exciting! Do tell.

Crane (*severely*). Such dreadful horrors are not for the ears of the gentler sex, Miss Van Tassel. They would frighten you.

Katrina. But I just love terrifying stories of witches and ghosts and goblins. We have lots of those here in Sleepy Hollow. You've heard of the Headless Horseman, haven't you?

Crane. Certainly, Miss Van Tassel. But of course I don't believe in such absurd local superstitions.

Katrina. But it's perfectly true! Why, often at night my shutters have rattled as he galloped by my bedroom window on his great dark ghost horse. It's quite thrilling.

Crane (*nervously*). I'm sure it's just the wind, Miss Van Tassel.

Katrina. Oh, no, Mr. Crane. I've seen his shadow on my wall as he passed.

Crane. Surely just a farmer, hurrying home late from town to his warm hearth and a hearty supper.

Katrina. Without his head?

[CRANE *shudders.* BROM VAN BRUNT *enters from behind and claps his hand heavily on* CRANE's *shoulder.*]

Brom. Ichabod Crane!

[CRANE *screams and faints dead away.*]

Katrina. Mr. Crane!

[*She kneels by* CRANE *and fans his face.*]

Katrina. Brom, you great bully, how could you?

Brom. What did I do?

Katrina. You frightened poor Mr. Crane half to death.

Brom. That witless schoolteacher is afraid of his own shadow.

Katrina. He has a sensitive nature. It comes from spending his time thinking and reading, instead of roaring around the country on horseback stirring up trouble like some people I know.

Brom. Thinking and reading! I've never seen him read any book but that one. (*Picks it up*) Hah! Witches. Bunch of foolishness. (*Tosses it back down*) As for thinking, my guess is all he thinks about is the next meal he can sponge at your family's table.

Katrina. Brom Van Brunt, you're just jealous.

Brom. What if I am? We were practically planning our wedding before Ichabod Crane came along. Now you don't give me so much as a "Good afternoon."

[CRANE, *still lying on the floor, raises his head.*]

Brom. He's always sneaking around, cozying up to you when I'm away, running like a rabbit when he sees me coming. Why doesn't he stand and fight? I'll give your great thinker something to think about.

[*He makes a fist and punches his open palm.* CRANE *groans and drops back.*]

Katrina. Now, Brom, you silly old thing. Of course I still like you. Why, just this morning I was asking Papa if we could have you over to supper tomorrow night. Mama and I have been plucking pigeons for pigeon pie.

[*She takes his arm.* BROM, *mollified, allows her to lead him away. At the edge of the stage* KATRINA *turns back and calls to* CRANE, *who is beginning to stir.*]

Katrina. You're invited too, Mr. Crane!

Brom (*grumbling*). Better bake a dozen extra pies, then.

[*They exit.*]

Act Two

Next evening at the Van Tassels' home.

CRANE, KATRINA, *and* BROM *are sitting at the table with* KATRI-NA'S MOTHER *and* FATHER, *a kind, easygoing farm couple. They have just finished dessert.*

Mother. More coffee, anyone? Another cruller? Slice of peach pie, Mr. Crane? There's plenty left.

Crane. My dear Mrs. Van Tassel, I couldn't possibly eat another bite.

Brom. Now there's a weird and uncanny event. Only three plates of supper and two of dessert and he's already full. One of those New England witches must have put a hex on him.

Father. Eh? What's that?

Crane. I believe Mr. Van Brunt is alluding to my studies of the history of the supernatural in my birthplace, New England.

Father. Plenty of supernatural goings-on right here in Sleepy Hollow.

Katrina. That's what I told him, Papa.

Mother. Oh, yes, Mr. Crane. Have you seen the haunted bridge where Major John André was captured? Sometimes you can hear the most fearful groans when you ride over it.

Katrina. How about the woman in white who haunts the dark glen down by Raven Rock? They say she died there in a terrible blizzard. I've heard her myself, shrieking and wailing on cold winter nights when a storm is coming.

[CRANE *wipes his brow nervously.*]

Crane. Those are just tales to frighten children. Everyone knows there's no truth to them. Captured spies, women in white, headless horsemen . . .

Mother. Oh, but Mr. Crane. Folks around here have seen the Headless Horseman many a time.

Father. Old Brouwer never believed in him either. Not until the Headless Horseman came up behind him one night and yanked Brouwer right up into the saddle with him. Rode him all over creation, up hill and down, through bush and swamp.

Katrina. When they reached the haunted bridge, the Headless Horseman turned into a skeleton and threw poor Mr. Brouwer right into the brook. Then he sprang away over the treetops with a great clap of thunder. That's the way I heard it.

Brom. Come to that, I guess I've seen the Headless Horseman myself.

Katrina (*admiringly*). Brom, not really?

Brom. Why, sure. It was just last week.

Mother. Do tell, Brom!

[BROM *grins and leans back in his chair.*]

Brom. Well, Daredevil and I were on our way home from Tarrytown late one night—

Katrina. Daredevil! That great black beast is going to throw you someday, Brom.

Father. I don't know why anyone would keep such an evil-tempered horse.

Brom. That's why he's my favorite. Keeps the ride interesting. Anyway, he's fast. Fast enough to outrun any horse around these parts—in a *fair* race. But that headless Hessian is nothing but a cheat.

Crane. Cheat?

Brom. That's what I said, and I'll stand by it. Round about midnight he came trotting up behind me. Over by the haunted bridge, it was.

Katrina. Ooh! What happened, Brom?

Brom. Well, I'm always up for a bit of sport, so I challenged him to a race. Didn't even ask for a head start, though I'd been riding Daredevil hard since morning and that goblin horse of his was fresh from a nice restful day in the grave.

Mother. You tried to race the Headless Horseman?

Brom. *Did* race him. Would have won, too. I was ahead by a neck and gaining steady. But just as we passed the churchyard, that cheating Hessian bolted. Vanished in a flash of fire.

[KATRINA'S FATHER *bursts out laughing.*]

Father. Brom, you young scoundrel. The tales you tell.

Brom (*with mock seriousness*). So you see, *Mister* Crane, the Headless Horseman is altogether real and true. Could be you'll see him yourself on your way home tonight. I hope he won't scare you into dropping your *book* in the mud. Maybe you should sing a psalm or two if you want him to keep his distance. (*Leans toward* CRANE) Works on the rest of us.

Act Three
Later that night, on the road.

The scene is set with a white sheet or screen as a backdrop. The HEADLESS HORSEMAN *will appear as a shadow cast on the backdrop from behind. This effect may be achieved using, for example, an actor in front of a strong light or a black paper cut-out figure laid on an overhead projector.*

[CRANE *walks slowly along the road, glancing around nervously with every step. Suddenly the hooting of an owl is heard.* CRANE *jumps back and cries out in fear.*]

Crane (*recovering*). Oh. Just an owl. A harmless screech owl. Well, how was I to know? A noise like that would startle anyone.

[*He starts forward again and brushes his arm against a tree limb. He screams and crouches down, covering his head with his hands. After a moment he gathers his courage and peeks up.*]

Crane. Oh. Just a branch. A harmless tree branch. Perfectly natural mistake, though. Could happen to anyone.

[*He picks himself up and brushes himself off, embarrassed. He is just starting forward again when a sound is heard: the clip-clop of a horse's hooves approaching, still faint and in the distance.* CRANE *stops to listen.*]

Crane (*nervously*). It's just the wind. Nothing but the wind in the trees.

[*The sound of the horse's hooves gets louder.*]

Crane. It's just a farmer. Nothing but a farmer heading home late. I'll just move aside and let him pass by.

[*The sound of the horse's hooves gets even louder, then stops. The shadow of the* HEADLESS HORSEMAN *appears on the backdrop, looming over* CRANE, *who has his back to it. The* HEADLESS HORSEMAN *carries a round, head-sized object (such as a rubber kickball) on the saddle in front of him.*]

Crane (*without turning*). G-g-good evening, n-n-neighbor.

[*Silence.*]

Crane. P-p-please go r-r-right ahead, good n-n-neighbor. D-d-don't let me stand in your w-w-way.

[*Silence. Finally* CRANE *turns and sees the* HEADLESS HORSEMAN. *He starts, then shrinks away from him in terror.*]

Crane. Wh-wh-who are you?

[*Silence.*]

Crane. W-w-what do you want of me?

[*Silence.* CRANE's *legs buckle under him and he falls to his knees. He clasps his hands and bows his head.*]

Crane (*in a trembling voice*). "Yea, though I walk through the valley of the shadow of death, I shall fear no evil. For— For—"

[*Slowly, the* HEADLESS HORSEMAN *raises high the "head" in his hands. Slowly,* CRANE *lifts his head and looks at him. The* HEADLESS HORSEMAN *pulls back his arms, as if preparing to throw the "head." Then suddenly he heaves it toward the backdrop, which hangs between him and* CRANE. *At that moment, there is a crash and the lights go out.*]

[*A moment later, the lights go on. The* HEADLESS HORSEMAN *is gone.* CRANE *lies unconscious on the stage. The lights go out again.*]

Epilogue

The village inn, 1819.

The TRAVELERS *and the* INNKEEPER *are back at their places around the table.*

Innkeeper. And there you have it: the story of Ichabod Crane and the Headless Horseman.

[*He leans back and taps out his pipe.*]

Traveler 2 (*sarcastically*). So I suppose they found him lying there the next morning, dead of fright, of course. A look of indescribable horror frozen on his lifeless face.

Innkeeper. Oh, no. Nothing there to find.

Traveler 1. What happened to Crane?

Innkeeper. Some say Ichabod was carried away by the galloping Hessian.

Traveler 2. Now *that's* scary.

Traveler 1. What happened to Katrina?

Innkeeper. Oh, she married Brom Van Brunt. (*dreamily*) What a reception. Smoked beef. Stuffed turkey with sausages. Lovely quince jelly. Piles of ginger cakes. Hasn't been a wedding spread like that round these parts in years.

Traveler 2. Then she wasn't too disturbed by the fate of her other suitor?

Innkeeper. Disturbed? No. Funny thing, though. Seems like to this day, every time someone tells that story, Katrina gives Brom a most peculiar look. And he gives her the same look back. Some suspect they know more about the matter than they choose to tell.

Traveler 1. What happened the day after?

Innkeeper. Well, a couple of the farmers decided to take a ride down—in the daylight of course—and have a look at the scene. Did I tell you it all happened at the haunted bridge where Major André was captured?

Traveler 2 (*exclaims*). Where else?

Traveler 1. What did they find?

Innkeeper. No sign of Crane. But they did find something strange down there—a shattered pumpkin, lying in pieces all over the road. (*Pauses in reflection*) 'Course, I don't believe every story I hear. But they do say that the legend of Sleepy Hollow is absolutely true.

Washington Irving
(1783–1859)

Washington Irving was the first American writer to win respect from writers in Great Britain and continental Europe. Before Irving, people thought that Americans could produce only poor imitations of stories written abroad.

Washington Irving was born in New York City on the same day the American Revolution ended, and was named for George Washington. A small and sickly but bright child, Irving was the last of eleven children and the spoiled darling in the family of a successful hardware merchant.

Irving trained as a lawyer, but he came to loathe the drudgery of business, which he described as a "sordid, dusty, soul-killing way of life." Good-looking and witty, he loved nothing more than telling funny and satirical stories to his friends.

At twenty-one, Irving made his first trip to Europe. He filled notebooks with descriptions of his adventures, which included an escape from pirates, poor lodging, rough rides, and flirtations with beautiful women. When he returned, he joined other young men in publishing a humor magazine that poked fun at the manners and customs of the day.

Some years later, after working in Washington, D.C., Irving returned to Europe. There he decided to leave the world of business and devote himself to writing. In 1817, he began working on a series of stories and essays. These pieces, which include "Rip Van Winkle" and "The

Legend of Sleepy Hollow," became *The Sketch Book of Geoffrey Crayon, Gent.* (1819–1820), a book that made Irving his country's first internationally successful writer.

William Thackeray, the British novelist, called Irving "the first ambassador from the New World of letters . . . to the old." Irving enjoyed this role to the fullest. His writing, which was translated into several languages, was loved by readers of all ages, rich and poor. He even served as U.S. minister to Spain for four years.

Today we remember Irving as the creator of Rip Van Winkle, who slept through the American Revolution, and the Headless Horseman, who tormented the lovelorn schoolteacher Ichabod Crane. Irving's stories are now considered landmarks in American literature.

The Devil and Daniel Webster

Stephen Vincent Benét
dramatized by Mara Rockliff

Characters

Narrators (2)
Jabez Stone
The Devil
Daniel Webster
Justice Hathorne
Walter Butler

Optional: The other members of the jury (11 non-speaking parts)

Setting: New Hampshire and Massachusetts, the 1820s (told in flashback by narrator).

Prologue

Narrator 1. Yes, Dan'l Webster's dead—or, at least, they buried him. But every time there's a thunderstorm around Marshfield, Massachusetts, they say you can hear his rolling voice in the hollows of the sky. And they say that if you go to his grave and speak loud and clear, "Dan'l Webster! Dan'l Webster!" the ground will begin to shiver and the trees begin to shake. And after a while you'll hear a deep voice saying, "Neighbor, how stands the Union?" Then you better answer, "The Union stands

141

as it stood, rock bottomed and copper sheathed, one and indivisible." Otherwise, he's liable to rear right out of the ground. At least, that's what I was told when I was a youngster.

Narrator 2. You see, for a while, he was the biggest man in the country. He never got to be President, but he was the biggest man. They said, when he stood up to speak, stars and stripes came right out in the sky, and once he spoke against a river and made it sink into the ground. They said, when he walked in the woods with his fishing rod, Kill-all, the trout would jump out of the streams right into his pockets, for they knew it was no use putting up a fight against him. And when he argued a case, he could turn on the harps of the blessed and the shaking of the earth underground. A man with a mouth like a mastiff, a brow like a mountain and eyes like burning anthracite—that was Dan'l Webster in his prime. And the biggest case he argued never got written down in the books, for he argued it against the devil nip and tuck and no holds barred. And this is the way I used to hear it told.

Act One

Jabez Stone's farm

JABEZ STONE *is walking back and forth, plowing his field.*

Narrator 1. There was a man named Jabez Stone, lived at Cross Corners, New Hampshire. He wasn't a bad man to start with, but he was an unlucky man. He had good enough land, but it didn't prosper him. He had a decent wife and children, but the more children he had, the less there was to feed them. If he planted corn, he got borers. If he planted potatoes, he got blight. If stones cropped up in his neighbor's field, boulders boiled up in his. But one day Jabez Stone got sick of the whole business.

[STONE *suddenly stops short.*]

Stone. Whoa!

[*He bends down to look at the blade of the plow.*]

Stone (*angrily*). Broken!

[*He picks up something with both hands and heaves it aside.*]

Stone. I'd swear that rock wasn't there yesterday. (*sighs*) Now what am I going to do? My horse is sick, the kids have the measles, my poor old wife is ailing, and you know, I'm not feeling so good myself. Now my only plow is broken.

[*He kicks at it and stubs his toe.*]

Stone. Ouch! (*holding his foot*) This is the last straw. It's enough to make a man want to sell his soul to the devil. And I would, too, for two cents!

[*The* DEVIL *enters.*]

Devil (*suavely*). You called, Mr. Stone?
Narrator 2. Well, Jabez Stone didn't like the looks of this stranger. Stone was a religious man, and right away he wished he hadn't said what he'd said. But he was a New Hampshireman, too, and having given his word, more or less, he wouldn't take it back. So they went out behind the barn and made their bargain.

[*The* DEVIL *unrolls a long scroll and points to the bottom, then hands* STONE *a pin.* STONE *pantomimes jabbing his finger and signing in blood. The* DEVIL *rolls up the scroll and shakes* STONE'S *hand.*]

Devil. It's a pleasure doing business with you, Mr. Stone.

[*He exits.* STONE *looks at his plow.*]

Stone. Well, I'll be! Good as new. And if that horse doesn't look ten years younger, my name's not Jabez Stone.

[*He returns to his plowing, whistling happily.*]

Narrator 1. After that, things began to pick up and prosper for Jabez Stone. His cows got fat and his horses sleek. His crops were the envy of the neighborhood. And lightning might strike all over the valley, but it wouldn't strike his barn. Pretty soon, he was one of the richest people in the county. They began to talk of running him for state senate. All in all, you might say the Stone family was as happy and contented as cats in a dairy. And so they were, except for Jabez Stone.

Narrator 2. He'd been contented enough, the first few years. It's a great thing when bad luck turns. It drives most other things out of your head. But every now and then, especially in rainy weather, the little white scar on his finger would give him a twinge. And once a year, as punctual as clockwork, the stranger passed by his farm. But the sixth year, the stranger stayed, and after that, his peace was over for Jabez Stone.

[*The DEVIL enters, carrying a black briefcase or bag. STONE stops plowing. The DEVIL looks around approvingly.*]

Devil. Well Mr. Stone, you're a hummer! It's a very pretty property you've got here, Mr. Stone.

Stone. Well, some might favor it and others might not.

Devil (*smiles*). Oh, no need for your New Hampshire modesty! After all, we know what's been done, and it's all been according to contract and specifications. So when—ahem—the "mortgage" [*he winks at STONE*] falls due next year, you shouldn't have any regrets.

[STONE *looks around, and up at the sky.*]

Stone. Speaking of that mortgage, mister . . . I'm beginning to have one or two doubts about it.

Devil. Doubts? (*His smile fades.*)

Stone. Why, yes. This being the USA and me always having been a religious man. (*He clears his throat, then, more boldly.*) Yes, sir. I'm beginning to have considerable doubts as to that mortgage holding in court.

Devil. There's all kinds of courts, aren't there? Still, we might as well have a look at the original document.

[*He opens the black bag, pulls out a folder full of papers and leafs through it.*]

Devil. Sherwin, Slater, Stevens, Stone. "I, Jabez Stone, for a term of seven years"—oh, it's quite in order, I think.

[*From a tape recorder hidden in the open bag we hear a squeaky voice:* Neighbor Stone! Neighbor Stone! Help me! For God's sake, help me!

[STONE *looks at the bag in horror. The* DEVIL *hastily stuffs the folder back in the bag* (*turning off the tape recorder*) *and shuts the bag.*]

Devil. Sorry for the interruption. As I was saying—

Stone (*hoarsely*). That's Miser Stevens's voice! And you've got his soul in your bag!

Devil. Yes, I just picked him up on my way over—

Stone. He ain't dead! You can't tell me he is! He was just as spry and mean as a woodchuck on Tuesday!

[*The* DEVIL *folds his hands and bows his head as if in prayer.*]

Devil (*with mock piety*). In the midst of life, we are in death. . . . Listen!

[*A bell tolls.*]

Devil (*sighs*). These longstanding accounts. One really hates to close them. But business is business. See you in a year, Mr. Stone.

[*He picks up his bag and exits.* STONE *falls to his knees and prays.*]

Act Two

Daniel Webster's farm

STONE *and* DANIEL WEBSTER *are sitting together at a table, eating breakfast and talking.*

Narrator 1. The year seemed to pass in a moment for Jabez Stone. Every day when he got up, he thought, "There's one more night gone." And every night when he lay down, he thought of that black bag and the soul of Miser Stevens, and it made him sick at heart. Finally, he couldn't bear it any longer. On the very last day of his contract he hitched up his horse and drove off to seek Dan'l Webster. For Dan'l was born in New Hampshire, only a few miles from Cross Corners, and it was well known that he had a particular soft spot for old neighbors.

Narrator 2. It was early in the morning when he reached the big farm in Marshfield, but Dan'l was up already, talking Latin to the farmhands and wrestling with the ram, Goliath, and working up speeches to make against John C. Calhoun. But when he heard a New Hampshireman had come to see him, he dropped everything he was doing, for that was Dan'l's way. He gave Jabez Stone a breakfast that five men couldn't eat and went into the living history of every man and woman in Cross Corners. Then he asked what he could do for him, and Jabez Stone told him his story.

Webster. You've certainly given yourself the devil's own row to hoe, Neighbor Stone. But I'll take your case.

Stone. You'll take it?

Webster. Yes, I will. I've got about seventy-five other things to do and the Missouri Compromise to straighten out, but if I can, I'll help you.

Stone. Then I've got hope for the first time in seven years.

Narrator 1. So they sat and talked until the sun went down, and then they waited. The stranger was scheduled to show up on the stroke of midnight, wherever Jabez Stone might be, according to specifications.

Narrator 2. Well, most men wouldn't have asked for better company than Dan'l Webster. But with every tick of the clock Jabez Stone got sadder and sadder. Finally, on the stroke of 11:30 he reached over and grabbed Dan'l Webster by the arm.

Stone. Mr. Webster, Mr. Webster! (*his voice shaking with fear*) Mr. Webster, get away while you can!

Webster. You've come a long way, neighbor, to tell me you don't like my company.

Stone. Miserable wretch that I am! I've brought you a devilish way, and now I see my folly. Let him take me if he wills. I don't hanker after it, I must say, but I can stand it. But you're the Union's stay and New Hampshire's pride! He mustn't get *you*, Mr. Webster! He mustn't get you!

Webster (*gently*). I'm obliged to you, Neighbor Stone. It's kindly thought of. But there's a case in hand. And I never left a case half finished in my life.

[*There is a knock at the door.* WEBSTER *gets up and opens it.*]

Webster. Come in!

[*The* DEVIL *enters, carrying his black bag.* STONE *gives a low cry of fear and backs into the farthest corner of the room.*]

Devil. Mr. Webster, I presume.

Webster. Attorney of record for Jabez Stone. Might I ask your name?

Devil. I've gone by a good many. Perhaps Scratch will do for the evening. I'm often called that in these regions. (*smiles*) And now, I shall call upon you, as a law-abiding citizen, to assist me in taking possession of my property.

[*The* DEVIL *and* WEBSTER *pantomime their argument as the* NARRATORS *speak.* STONE *remains cowering silently in the corner.*]

Narrator 1. And with that the argument began—and it went hot and heavy. At first, Jabez Stone had a flicker of hope, but then he saw Dan'l Webster being forced back at point after point. For there wasn't any doubt as to the deed or signature—that was the worst of it. Dan'l Webster twisted and turned and thumped his fist on the table, but he couldn't get away from that.

Narrator 2. He offered to compromise the case, but the stranger wouldn't hear of it. He pointed out that the property had increased in value and state senators ought to be worth more, but the stranger stuck to the letter of the law. He was a great lawyer, was Dan'l Webster, but we know who's the King of Lawyers, as the Good Book tells us, and it seemed as if, for the first time, Dan'l Webster had met his match.

Devil (*yawns*). Your spirited efforts on behalf of your client do you credit, Mr. Webster. But if you have no more arguments, I'm rather pressed for time. . . .

Webster (*shouting*). Pressed or not, you shall not have this man! Mr. Stone is an American citizen, and no American citizen may be forced into the service of a foreign prince. We fought England for that in 1812 and we'll fight all Hell for it again!

Devil. Foreign? And who calls me a foreigner?

Webster (*surprised*). Well, I never heard yet of the dev—of your claiming American citizenship.

Devil (*with an evil smile*). And who with better right?

When the first wrong was done to the first Indian, I was there. When the first slave ship set sail for the Congo, I stood on its deck. Am I not in your books and stories and beliefs, from the first settlements on? Am I not spoken of, still, in every church in New England? It's true the North says I'm a Southerner and the South says I'm a Northerner, but I am neither. I am merely an honest American like yourself, and of the best descent. For, though I don't like to boast of it, my name is older in this country than yours.

Webster. Aha! Then I stand on the Constitution! I demand a trial for my client!

Devil (*nervously*). The case is hardly one for an ordinary court. And, indeed, the lateness of the hour—

Webster. Let it be any court you choose, so long as it is an American judge and an American jury! Let them be living or dead, I'll argue my case before them.

Devil. You have said it.

[*He points at the door. We hear the sound of heavy footsteps approaching.*]

Stone (*terrified*). In God's name, who comes by so late?

Devil. The jury Mr. Webster demands. You must pardon the rough appearance of one or two. They have come a long way.

[*The door opens and twelve people march in grimly and take their places as the* NARRATORS *speak.*]

Narrator 1. If Jabez Stone had been sick with terror before, he was blind with terror now.

Narrator 2. For there was Walter Butler, the loyalist, who spread fire and horror through the Mohawk valley in the times of the Revolution. There was the Wampanoag chief King Phillip, with the great gash in his head that gave him his death wound, and cruel Governor Dale, who broke men on the wheel in colonial Virginia. There was Teach, the bloody pirate, and the Reverend John Smeet, with his strangler's hands and the red mark of the gallows rope still on his neck.

Narrator 1. One and all, they came into the room with the fires of Hell still upon them, and the stranger named their names and their deeds as they came, till the tale of twelve was told. Yet the stranger had told the truth—they had all played a part in America.

Devil. Are you satisfied with the jury, Mr. Webster?

Webster (*bravely*). Quite satisfied. Though I miss General Arnold from the company.

Devil. Benedict Arnold is engaged upon other business. Ah, you asked for a judge, I believe.

[*He points his finger again.* JUSTICE HATHORNE *enters and take his place.*]

Devil. Justice Hathorne is a judge of experience. He presided at certain witch trials once held in Salem. There were others who repented of the business later, but not he.

Hathorne. Repent of such notable wonders and undertakings? Nay, hang them all. Hang them all!

[STONE *faints. The other characters begin to pantomime the trial as the* NARRATORS *speak.*]

Narrator 1. Dan'l Webster had faced some hard juries and hanging judges in his time, but this was the hardest he'd ever faced, and he knew it. They sat there with a kind of glitter in their eyes, and the stranger's smooth voice went on and on. Every time he'd raise an objection, it'd be "Objection sustained," but whenever Dan'l objected, it'd be "Objection denied." Well, you couldn't expect fair play from a fellow like Mr. Scratch.

Narrator 2. It got to Dan'l in the end, and he began to heat, like iron in the forge. When he got up to speak he was going to flay that stranger with every trick known to the law, and the judge and jury too. He didn't care if it was contempt of court or what would happen to him for it. He didn't care any more what happened to Jabez Stone. He just got madder and madder, thinking of what he'd say. And yet, curiously enough, the more he thought about it, the less he was able to arrange his speech in his mind.

Narrator 1. Finally it was time for him to come forward, and he did so, all ready to burst out with lightning and denunciations. But before he started, he looked at the judge and jury. And he noticed the glitter in their eyes was twice as strong as before, and they all leaned forward. Then he saw what he'd been about to do, and he wiped his forehead, as someone might who's just escaped falling into a pit in the dark.

Narrator 2. For it was him they'd come for, not just Jabez Stone. And if he fought them with their own weapons, he'd fall into their power. It was his own anger and horror that burned in their eyes, and he'd have to wipe that out or the case was lost. He stood there for a moment, and then he began to speak.

Narrator 1. He talked about the things that made a country a country, and human beings human. He began with the simple things that everyone's known and felt—the freshness of a fine morning, and the taste of food when you're hungry, and the new day that's every day when you're a child.

Narrator 2. Then he talked about the early days of America. He admitted all the wrong that had ever been done. But he showed how out of the wrong and the right, the suffering and the starvation, something new had come. And everybody had played a part in it, even the traitors.

Narrator 1. Then he turned to Jabez Stone and showed him as he was—an ordinary man who'd had hard luck and wanted to change it. And now he was going to be punished for all eternity. As he went on, Dan'l wasn't pleading for one person anymore. He was telling the story and the failures and the endless journey of humankind. They got tricked and trapped and bamboozled, but it was a great journey. And no demon that was ever foaled could know what it was to be human.

Narrator 2. And when Dan'l Webster finished, he didn't know whether or not he'd saved Jabez Stone. But he knew he'd done a miracle. For the glitter was gone from the eyes of judge and jury, and for the moment they were human again, and knew they were human.

Webster. The defense rests.

Hathorne. The jury will retire to consider its verdict.

[*Walter Butler steps forward.*]

Butler. The jury has considered its verdict. We find for the defendant, Jabez Stone. Perhaps it's not strictly in accordance with the evidence, but even the damned may salute the eloquence of Mr. Webster.

[*The* JUDGE *and jury exit. The* DEVIL *shakes his head and turns to* WEBSTER, *holding the scroll with* STONE's *contract.*]

Devil. Major Butler was always a bold man. I had not thought him quite so bold. Nevertheless, my congratulations, as between two gentlemen.

Webster. I'll have that paper first, if you please. (*He tears it up.*) And now, I'll have you!

[*He grabs the* DEVIL *by the arm. The* DEVIL *tries unsuccessfully to twist away.*]

Devil. Now, now, Mr. Webster. This sort of thing is—

ouch!—is ridiculous. If you're worried about the costs of the case, naturally, I'd be glad to pay . . .

Webster. And so you shall! (*shaking him*) For you'll sit right down at that table and draw up a document, promising never to bother Jabez Stone nor his family nor any other New Hampshireman till doomsday! For any Hell we want to raise in this part of the country, we can raise ourselves, without assistance from strangers.

Devil. Ouch! All right. I agree.

[*They sit down and the* DEVIL *writes.*]

Devil. And, now, may I go?

Webster. Go? I'm still trying to figure out what I'll do with you. For you've settled the costs of the case, but you haven't settled with me. I think I'll take you back to my farm. I've got a ram there named Goliath that can butt through an iron door. I'd kind of like to turn you loose in his field and see what he'd do.

Narrator 1. Well, with that the Devil began to beg and to plead. And he begged and he pled so humble that finally Dan'l, who was naturally kindhearted, agreed to let him go. The Devil seemed terrible grateful for that and said, just to show they were friends, he'd tell Dan'l's fortune before leaving. So Dan'l agreed to that, though he didn't take much stock in fortunetellers ordinarily. But, naturally, the Devil was a little different.

[*The* DEVIL *takes his hand and examines the palm. He smiles.*]

Devil. The future's not what you think. It's dark. You have a great ambition, Mr. Webster.

Webster. Yes, I do.

Devil. It seems almost within your grasp, but you will not attain it. Lesser men will be made President and you will be passed over.

Webster. And if I am, I'll still be Dan'l Webster. What else?

Devil. You have two strong sons. You expect a long line of descendants. But your sons will both die in war and neither will reach greatness.

Webster. Live or die, they're still my sons. What else?

Devil. You have made great speeches. You will make more.

Webster. Ah.

Devil. But the last great speech you make will turn many of your own against you. Even in New England, some will say you have turned your coat and sold your country, and their voices will be loud against you until you die.

Webster. So long as it is an honest speech, it doesn't matter what people say. (*He looks at the* DEVIL.) One question. I have fought for the Union all my life. Will I see that fight won against those who try to tear it apart?

Devil. Not while you live, but it will be won. And after you are dead, there are thousands who will fight for your cause, because of words that you spoke.

Webster (*happily*). Why, then you long-barreled, slab-sided, lantern-jawed, fortune telling note shaver! Be off to your own place before I kick you there myself! For, by the thirteen original colonies, I'd go to Hell itself to save the Union!

[*He pushes the* DEVIL *out the door.* STONE *begins to revive from his faint.*]

Webster. And now, let's see what there is to drink around here. It's dry work talking all night. I hope there's pie for breakfast, Neighbor Stone.

Stephen Vincent Benét
(1898–1943)

Critics consider "The Devil and Daniel Webster" to be the best of several stories Stephen Vincent Benét wrote about Daniel Webster. First published in a popular magazine, *The Saturday Evening Post,* it was more successful than any of the stories Benét had published previously.

In many ways, Daniel Webster represented the ideal of patriotism that was most important to Benét. "We Benéts are an army family" was how Benét summed up the values of duty, honor, and love of country that his father had instilled in him as a child. During World War II, Benét lectured and wrote radio plays and speeches to rally support for the United States and its allies. He always refused to accept money for such work. Despite poor health, he worked tirelessly for the American cause and died suddenly of a heart attack while still in his mid-forties. He did not live to see the end of the war.

Benét's father had been a West Point graduate and a career army officer. His grandfather had also been in the military. Yet Stephen and his brother, William Rose Benét, chose career paths that broke family tradition. They and their sister, Laura, became writers. That decision probably did not surprise their parents. Stephen's parents often read poetry and history to their three children, who all started writing when they were quite young. At the age of thirteen, Stephen won his first literary prize, three dollars, in a poetry contest for children. When he was twenty-two, he won a Yale fellowship for study at the Sorbonne in France. While in Paris, he met his future wife, Rosemary Carr, who was also a writer. They collaborated in writing *A Book of Americans,* poems about real and legendary American heroes.

Benét was celebrated equally for his stories and poems. He won the Pulitzer Prize in 1929 for *John Brown's Body* (1929). This narrative poem about the events leading up to the Civil War was based partly on his father's collection of old military records. Shortly before Benét died, he completed the first section of *Western Star,* a five-volume poetic narrative of early settlement in America. His brother edited the work for publication; it won a second Pulitzer prize for Stephen Vincent Benét, awarded in 1944 after his death.

The Man Without a Country

Edward Everett Hale
dramatized by Mara Rockliff

Characters

Narrator
Philip Nolan
Colonel Morgan
The marshal (not a speaking part)
Two sailors
A young naval officer
Mrs. Graff
The captain
Lieutenant Vaughan
A sailor

Extras
Several army officers (Act One)
A group of sailors (Act Two)
Guests at the ball (Act Three)
Miscellaneous sailors (Act Four)
Several sailors and a lot of Africans (Act Five)

Setting: The 1800s, in the United States and at sea.

Prologue

The NARRATOR walks onstage reading a folded-open newspaper. He stops front and center, his attention still on the paper, then shakes his head and sighs.

Narrator (*reading*). "Philip Nolan. Died at sea, on board the U.S. ship *Levant*. May 11, 1863."

[*Looks up at the audience.*]

Narrator. Such a plain little announcement. And so his death matches his life: quiet, obscure, unnoticed. It might have been a great headline: GONE AT LAST—THE MAN WITHOUT A COUNTRY.

For fifty long years the press has known nothing of Philip Nolan, and neither, of course, has the public at large. The military protects its own, and in this case rightly so. To remain unknown was the one small mercy Philip Nolan could ask, after he'd lost everything else that had ever mattered to him.

But now he's gone. They buried him at sea. Even in death he could not hope to return to the country he'd come to hold so dear. There is no longer any reason to keep his secret. The story of Philip Nolan should be made known. Young Americans of today must learn, before it's too late, what it is to be—"a man without a country."

Act One
Fort Adams, Louisiana, 1807

A military court-martial is taking place. At one end of a long table, PHILIP NOLAN *slumps in his chair, defeated. Stern old* COLONEL MORGAN *sits at the other end. The places between them are filled with other officers of the United States Army. The* MARSHAL *stands guard by the door.*

Morgan. Lieutenant Nolan, this court martial was called for a most serious reason. You have been accused of treason against the United States of America. The evidence we have seen today is very incriminating. When Aaron

Burr visited this garrison recently, you were seen several times in his company. Your own men testified that for over a year you've been writing letters to this man, a known traitor—

Nolan. But, Colonel, all he did was buy some land here in Louisiana and make plans to bring settlers down.

Morgan. Settlers! An army is more like it. An army to conquer Mexico for his personal glory and power, an army to take over the western territories and turn them against the Union—

Nolan (*desperately*). None of those rumors were proved. The court in Richmond found him not guilty—

Morgan. A civilian court, with civilian lawyers who know how to stretch the truth thin enough to push it through any loophole they can find. You are under military law here, Lieutenant Nolan, and you will be held to a higher standard of behavior. (*pauses*) But in the military we temper justice with mercy. Is there anything you can say to show this court that you have been faithful to the United States?

[NOLAN *leaps to his feet angrily and hits the table with his fist.*]

Nolan. Damn the United States! I wish I may never hear of the United States again!

[*There is a shocked silence in the room.* NOLAN *slowly sinks back into his seat.*]

Morgan. Young man, half the officers you see here risked their lives in the Revolution that gave birth to this country—a birth that took place before your own. How dare you insult them and the memory of their fallen comrades?

[*He stares at* NOLAN, *who is frightened but keeps stubbornly silent.*]

Morgan. Well, you shall have your wish. Lieutenant Philip Nolan, you have been found guilty of treason. Here is your sentence. The court decides, subject to the approval of the President, that you may never again hear the name of the United States.

[NOLAN *laughs, but the laughter dies away as he looks around at the grim faces of the other officers.* MORGAN *looks to the* MARSHAL.]

Morgan. Marshal, you will take the prisoner to Orleans and deliver him to the naval commander there. Ask him to place Lieutenant Nolan aboard a ship bound on a long cruise. His clothing, food rations, and living quarters should be in every way possible those of an officer. No restraints should be placed on him except what is necessary to prevent his escape. But he must never, never be allowed to hear or read anything at all about the United States.

[*The* MARSHAL *takes* NOLAN *away.*]

Act Two
Aboard a U.S. Navy ship at sea

NOLAN *sits in a chair. A group of sailors sit some distance away on the deck, talking and laughing together.* NOLAN *picks up a newspaper that lies folded next to his chair.*

Nolan. Foreign, of course. Nothing but foreign newspapers for the man without a country. Can't risk having me see any mention of the United States. Not an article, not even so much as an advertisement. Well, a foreign paper is better than nothing, I suppose.

[*He sighs and opens the newspaper. A big hole has been cut out of the middle of the page. He throws the paper back on the deck in disgust.*]

Nolan. Oh, what's the use?

[*He buries his head in his hands. One of the sailors looks over at* NOLAN.]

Sailor 1. Look at poor old Plain Buttons. Now there's a sad sight.
Sailor 2. Who's that? Why do you call him Plain Buttons?
Sailor 1. He's an army lieutenant, but he's got plain buttons on his uniform instead of the regular ones that say "U.S.A." on 'em. He's a prisoner of some kind. We're never supposed to mention the United States when he's around.
Sailor 2. Why, what did he do?
Sailor 1. I don't know, but it must have been something awful. He's been out at sea for years now. When one ship's done with its tour, they pass him on to another one. The way I hear it is, he's never going home.
Sailor 2 (*sympathetically*). Poor sap. I've only been out here six months, and sometimes I feel like I'll never see home again. Let's see if he wants to come sit with us.

[*He walks over to* NOLAN.]

Sailor 2. Excuse me, sir, . . . uh . . . some of us fellows over there were just looking at some new books the captain picked up in the last port, and we thought you might want to come read with us for a bit. (*helpfully*) They're all limey books, sir, not Amer—I mean, they're all right, I think.
Nolan (*sadly*). Thank you, son. I'd be honored to join you.

[*They go over to the others and sit down.* SAILOR 1 *hands* NOLAN *an open book.*]

Sailor 1. Here's some poetry. Old-fashioned stuff—Sir Walter Scott. Captain says it's quite good. We've just been passing it around, reading aloud. Like to take the next turn, sir?

[*He points to the place and* NOLAN *begins to read.*]

Nolan. "Breathes there a man with soul so dead,
    Who never to himself hath said,
    This is my own, my native land!"

[*He stops and glances at the sailors, who stare at the deck, embarrassed.* NOLAN *continues slowly.*]

Nolan. "Whose heart hath ne'er within him burned,
    As home his footsteps he hath turned
    From wandering on a foreign strand!
    If such there breathe—"

[*His voice breaks. He jumps to his feet, flings the book overboard, and runs offstage. The sailors look accusingly at* SAILOR 1, *who spreads his hands helplessly: He didn't know. The* NARRATOR *enters.*]

Narrator. Nolan was never the same after that. Before, he would try to make light of his imprisonment, pretend to enjoy the voyage, and all that. But now the true meaning of his life sentence sank in. From that moment on he had the nervous, tired look of a heartsick man. He very seldom spoke unless he was spoken to. And he never read aloud again.

Act Three
A shipboard ballroom

Couples are dancing. A young NAVAL OFFICER *with a drink in his hand stands talking to* NOLAN.

Officer. Nice party, eh, Lieutenant? It was good of the captain to invite all these folks from the embassy aboard ship—especially the ladies. After all these weeks we've been tied up here in the harbor, it's about time for a party.
Nolan. I'm the only one who's been tied up in the harbor. The rest of you have been going ashore every day. Anyway, you don't have to pretend you came over to chat with me. I know you're here to keep an eye on me, make sure no one talks to me about the United States. (*sadly*) I don't blame you. You're just doing your job.
Officer (*embarrassed*). Nolan, I'm sorry—
Nolan. Look!
Officer. What?
Nolan. That woman—
Officer. Ah, Mrs. Graff. She's from—I mean, she's beautiful, isn't she?
Nolan. I know her. That's Emily Rutledge. I met her in Philadelphia.

[*He starts toward her.*]

Officer. Nolan, wait—

[NOLAN *ignores him and approaches* MRS. GRAFF.]

Nolan. I hope you have not forgotten me, Miss Rutledge. May I have the honor of dancing?
Mrs. Graff (*laughs*). I am not Miss Rutledge any longer, Mr. Nolan. But I will dance all the same.

[*She nods to the* OFFICER *and turns away with* NOLAN. *They begin to dance.*]

Nolan (*with studied casualness*). So, what do you hear from home, Mrs. Graff?

[MRS. GRAFF *stops dancing and draws back, highly offended.*]

Mrs. Graff (*haughtily*). Home! Mr. Nolan! I thought you were the man who never wanted to hear of home again!

[*She sweeps off, leaving* NOLAN *staring after her with a stricken expression on his face.*]

Act Four

The War of 1812

As the NARRATOR *talks,* NOLAN *and the other characters pantomime the action, stepping forward for their turns at dialogue.*

Narrator. The War of 1812 came along soon after that. In one of the great battles with the English, the ship Nolan was on took a bad hit with a cannonball. It came in a port-hole and took down the officer of the gun himself and almost every man of the gun's crew. It was not a nice thing to see. But Nolan stepped right in, loading the gun with his own hands and giving orders as if he were in charge.

[*The* CAPTAIN *walks by.* NOLAN *salutes.*]

Nolan. I'm just showing these boys how we used to do it in the artillery, sir.

Captain. I see you are, sir, and I thank you, sir. And I never shall forget this day, sir, and you never shall either, sir.

Narrator. Nolan stayed with the men, leading them and encouraging them, until the enemy ship lowered its flag in defeat. And when the battle was won, the captain called Nolan forward.

Captain. Mr. Nolan, we are all very grateful to you today. You are one of us today.

Narrator. Nolan cried like a baby that day, and well he might. He hadn't worn a sword since that terrible day at Fort Adams. (*pauses*) The captain wrote a special letter to the secretary of war, too, asking for Nolan to be pardoned. But nothing ever came of it.

Act Five

Aboard a slave ship

LIEUTENANT VAUGHAN *stands on a barrel, surrounded by* AFRICANS *in chains, all talking to him at once in different languages. Several* SAILORS *are working to remove the chains from the* AFRICANS' *wrists and ankles. The* NARRATOR *steps forward.*

Narrator. About eight years after the war with the English, Nolan was on a ship cruising off the western coast of Africa when they overtook a schooner carrying kidnapped Africans to be sold into slavery. An officer named Vaughan was sent aboard to take charge of the ship and tell the people they were free.
Vaughan (*looking down at the confusion*). You're all free now! Free! (*desperately*) Can't anyone help me make these poor people understand something?

[NOLAN *enters, looking older than when we saw him last.*]

Nolan. I speak a bit of Portuguese, sir. Perhaps I can be of help.

[NOLAN *pantomimes speaking to the crowd. Several* AFRICANS *step forward, nodding eagerly.*]

Vaughan. Tell them they are free.

[NOLAN *speaks to the* AFRICAN *translators, who turn and relay the news to others. The news spreads through the crowd and there is an uproar of happiness: laughing, shouting, hugging, etc.*]

Vaughan (*pleased*). Tell them I'll take them all to Cape Palmas.

[NOLAN *turns and speaks, and as the news spreads the uproar of happiness dies, turning to head shaking, sobbing, etc.*]

Vaughan (*surprised*). Well, what's wrong now?

[NOLAN *confers with his translators, then turns to* VAUGHAN, *his voice shaking with emotion.*]

Nolan. These people are from the other side of the continent, sir, thousands of miles from Cape Palmas. They say, "Take us home to our own country. Take us to our own families." This man (*he gestures*) says he has an old father and mother who will die if they don't see him again. And this one (*he gestures*) says that he left his people sick, and paddled down to find a doctor to help them, and these devils kidnapped him, and he has never seen anyone from home since then. (*pauses*) If you drop them at Cape Palmas, they say, they— (*his voice breaks*) they will never see home again.

[VAUGHAN *is overcome with sympathy.*]

Vaughan. Yes, yes. Tell them yes. I'll take them to the Mountains of the Moon if I have to. If I have to sail this schooner through the Great White Desert, these people will go home!

[NOLAN *turns again to the crowd, who become joyful again. But* NOLAN *walks sadly to the rail and leans on it, staring out at the sea. One of the* SAILORS *walks over, and* NOLAN *turns to him.*]

Nolan. Son, let that show you what it is to be without a family, without a home, and without a country. Always think of your home. Let it be nearer and nearer to your thought the farther you have to travel from it, and rush back to it when you are free, as those poor slaves are doing now.

Sailor. Y-yes, sir. I—

Nolan. And as for your country, never dream of anything but serving it, though the service carry you through a thousand hells. Remember that behind all your officers, and the government, and the people, even, there is the country itself, your country, and you belong to it as you belong to your own mother. Stand by it, boy, as you would stand by your mother!

Sailor. Yes, sir. Of course. I—

Nolan (*in despair*). Oh, if anyone had said so to me when I was your age!

Epilogue

Narrator. I was that young sailor. I never saw Nolan again after that voyage, but I never forgot his words to me. (*sighs*) And now he's gone. They say as he lay on his deathbed, he begged the captain of the *Levant* to speak to him at last of the United States. Knowing he was dying, the captain told him everything—all that had happened in over fifty years. He pointed to the stars on the flag and talked about all the new states that had joined the Union, from Louisiana to Oregon. He told him about the invention of the steamboat, and the telegraph, and the railroad that stretched across a nation that was so much bigger than the one Nolan had left behind. He told him about all the Presidents, down to the latest, Abraham Lincoln.

Then the captain and Nolan prayed together, for themselves and for their country.

[*Pulls a note from his pocket and reads it.*]

Narrator. After Nolan died, they found this slip of paper on the table beside his bed. This is what he wrote: "Bury me in the sea. It has been my home, and I love it. But won't someone set up a stone for my memory? Say on it: 'In memory of Philip Nolan, Lieutenant in the Army of the United States. He loved his country as no other man has loved her. But no man deserved less at her hands.'"

[*The* NARRATOR *puts the note back in his pocket and exits.*]

Edward Everett Hale
(1822–1909)

"Look up and not down, look forward and not back, look out and not in, and lend a hand." That was the charitable philosophy of the main character in a series of stories called *Ten Times One Is Ten* written by Edward Everett Hale. A highly respected clergyman, journalist, magazine editor, and teacher, Hale was the first to express that motto, "Lend a hand," and he lived by it all his life.

Hale had one famous relative on each side of his family. His father's uncle (his own great-uncle) was Nathan Hale (1755–1776), martyr of the American Revolution. On the gallows, just before the British hanged him as a spy, Nathan Hale said, "I only regret that I have but one life to lose for my country." One of Edward's mother's brothers was Edward Everett (1794–1865), a Massachusetts statesman and orator who traveled throughout the North speaking for the Union cause during the Civil War. Everett's patriotism was overshadowed by his misfortune of being chosen to deliver a two-hour speech at Gettysburg, Pennsylvania, to dedicate the Soldiers Monument at the National Cemetery. Today nobody remembers what Everett said because he was followed by President Abraham Lincoln, who delivered the two-minute speech that became the enduring expression of our national purpose.

In addition to his famous relatives, Edward Everett Hale had every cultural advantage available to a member of wealthy, well-educated families of the time. He graduated from Harvard University at the age of seventeen, the youngest member of the class. He had grown up writing for the family newspaper, Boston's *The Daily Advertiser.*

Hale chose to pursue a career in the ministry, but he believed that the divinity schools of the time restricted freedom of thought. Instead of attending a divinity school, he studied religion on his own. He became pastor of the South Congregational Church in Boston in 1856, a position he held for forty-five years. He was appointed chaplain of the U.S. Senate in 1903.

Hale was one of the New England ministers most active in the antislavery movement. He did not serve in the Civil War, but he took such an active role in it that his likeness is on the Soldiers' Monument in Boston Common.

Hale believed that every work of fiction should have a serious purpose. If it exists only to entertain, he said, it is not worth reading. He liked to begin his short stories with a situation that could never happen in real life. Then he would make what followed seem so real that readers could not tell if they were reading a fictional story or a factual account. In 1863, Hale anonymously published his best-known story, "The Man Without a Country," to try to inspire patriotism during the Civil War. The story became very popular as a blend of fiction and history.

Hale was not an outstanding preacher or theologian, but he tirelessly devoted himself to public service to a degree unusual for most pastors of his day. Long before the days of privately or federally funded services to aid the needy, Hale advocated doing good for others. He worked for many social reforms, including better public education and low-cost housing. He was instrumental in the formation of several charitable organizations and was one of the first Americans to work for world peace.

The Wreck of the *Hesperus*

Henry Wadsworth Longfellow

NARRATOR 1   It was the schooner *Hesperus*,
      That sailed the wintry sea;
  And the skipper had taken his little
        daughter
      To bear him company.

DAUGHTER   Blue were her eyes as the fairy flax,   5
      Her cheeks like the dawn of day,
  And her bosom white as the hawthorn
        buds
      That ope in the month of May.

SKIPPER   The skipper he stood beside the helm,
      His pipe was in his mouth,   10
  And he watched how the veering flaw
        did blow
      The smoke now west, now south.

NARRATOR 1   Then up and spake an old sailor,
      Had sailed to the Spanish Main,
SAILOR   "I pray thee, put into yonder port,   15
      For I fear a hurricane.

  "Last night, the moon had a golden ring,
      And tonight no moon we see!"

SKIPPER   The skipper, he blew a whiff from his
                pipe,
            And a scornful laugh laughed he.   20

NARRATOR 2   Colder and louder blew the wind,
                A gale from the northeast,
            The snow fell hissing in the brine,
                And the billows frothed like yeast.

            Down came the storm, and smote
                amain   25
                The vessel in its strength;
            She shuddered and paused, like a
                frightened steed,
                Then leaped her cable's length.

SKIPPER   "Come hither! come hither! my little
                daughter,
                And do not tremble so;   30
            For I can weather the roughest gale
                That ever wind did blow."

NARRATOR 2   He wrapped her in his seaman's coat
                Against the stinging blast;
            He cut a rope from a broken spar,   35
                And bound her to the mast.

DAUGHTER   "O father! I hear the church bells ring;
                Oh, say, what may it be?"

SKIPPER   "'Tis a fog bell on a rock-bound coast!"
                And he steered for the open sea.   40

DAUGHTER   "O father! I hear the sound of guns;

Oh, say what may it be?"

SKIPPER   "Some ship in distress, that cannot live
    In such an angry sea!"

DAUGHTER   "O father! I see a gleaming light;   45
    Oh, say, what may it be?"

NARRATOR 2   But the father answered never a word,
    A frozen corpse was he.

Lashed to the helm, all stiff and stark,
    With his face turned to the skies,   50
The lantern gleamed through the
    gleaming snow
    On his fixed and glassy eyes.

NARRATOR 1   Then the maiden clasped her hands and
    prayed
    That saved she might be;
And she thought of Christ, who stilled
    the wave   55
    On the Lake of Galilee.

And fast through the midnight dark and
    drear,
    Through the whistling sleet and snow,
Like a sheeted ghost, the vessel swept
    Toward the reef of Norman's Woe.   60

And ever the fitful gusts between,
    A sound came from the land;
It was the sound of the trampling surf
    On the rocks and the hard sea sand.

The breakers were right beneath her
　　　bows,　　　　　　　　　　　　　65
　　She drifted a dreary wreck,
And a whooping billow swept the crew
　　Like icicles from her deck.

NARRATOR 2　She struck where the white and fleecy
　　　waves
　　Looked soft as carded wool,　　　70
But the cruel rocks, they gored her side
　　Like the horns of an angry bull.

Her rattling shrouds, all sheathed in ice,
　　With the masts went by the board;
Like a vessel of glass, she stove and
　　　sank;　　　　　　　　　　　　75
　　Ho! ho! the breakers roared!

At daybreak, on the bleak sea beach,
　　A fisherman stood aghast,
To see the form of a maiden fair,
　　Lashed close to a drifting mast.　80

The salt sea was frozen on her breast,
　　The salt tears in her eyes;
And he saw her hair, like the brown
　　　seaweed,
　　On the billows fall and rise.

NARRATORS 1　Such was the wreck of the *Hesperus*,　85
AND 2　　　In the midnight and the snow!
Christ save us all from a death like this,
　　On the reef of Norman's Woe!

Henry Wadsworth Longfellow
(1807–1882)

Not long ago almost every schoolchild in America could recite some of Henry Wadsworth Longfellow's poems by heart. Many of those memorized poems were long ones like "Paul Revere's Ride," which has more than 130 lines. *The Song of Hiawatha* and *The Courtship of Miles Standish* are even longer poems that have become part of our national heritage. They show Longfellow's talent for using American history and legends as background for poems of action and romance.

Henry Wadsworth Longfellow was and still is the most popular poet America has ever had. His popularity brought him "household name" status, and in 1841, his *Ballads and Other Poems* (including "The Wreck of the *Hesperus*") took the nation by storm. People eagerly awaited each new poem, and his works were translated into twenty-four languages. He lived during a time when people looked to poetry for comfort, spiritual uplift, and colorful accounts of historical subjects. Longfellow gave his readers all three.

Longfellow was fortunate to be born into a wealthy family that valued books and music. He grew up in Maine and was never far in his youth from the waves and rocks of the Atlantic coast. He graduated first in his class from Bowdoin College, which his grandfather had helped found.

After graduation, Longfellow spent four years in Europe, traveling and learning to speak French, Spanish, Italian, German, and Portuguese. He not only became an excellent linguist but also gained an understanding of

European culture, which his writing later communicated to Americans. On later trips to Europe, he learned Swedish, Danish, Icelandic, Dutch, and Finnish.

In 1835, after the tragic death of his first wife, Longfellow became a professor of French and Spanish at Harvard. Eight years later, he married Frances Appleton; they had five children and lived together happily for eighteen years. Longfellow produced some of his most celebrated poetry during these years. By 1854, his poetry was bringing in enough money that he could retire and devote himself fully to writing. But a second tragedy almost destroyed Longfellow's desire to create. His wife, Frances, died in a fiery accident at home when a candle ignited her summer dress. Longfellow tried to save her by smothering the flames with a rug and was badly burned himself.

Many of Longfellow's poems deal with nature, love of children, and love of country. They usually contain a moral lesson or sentiment that makes some of them seem dated for our times. He experimented with various types of narrative verse and ballads, adapting European forms to American subjects. (The rhythms of *The Song of Hiawatha* come from a Finnish epic poem.) Today, you'll still see in writing and even hear in conversation many phrases from his poems: "the patter of little feet," "the forest primeval," "ships that pass in the night," "the sands of time," "into each life some rain must fall."

Some years after his death, the English unveiled a memorial to Longfellow in the Poets' Corner of Westminster Abbey, where famous English writers, including Geoffrey Chaucer, William Shakespeare, Charles Dickens, Jane Austen, Charlotte Brontë, and Alfred, Lord Tennyson, are buried or memorialized. Longfellow was the first American poet to be so honored.

Robin Hood and Little John

1ST CHORUS	When Robin Hood was about twenty years old,
2ND CHORUS	*With a hey down, down, and a down;*
1ST CHORUS	He happened to meet Little John,
	A jolly brisk blade, right fit for the trade,
	For he was a lusty young man. 5

[2ND CHORUS	Though he was called Little, his limbs they were large
TO DO REFRAIN	And his stature was seven foot high;
THROUGHOUT°]	Wherever he came, they quaked at his name,
	For soon he would make them to fly.

How they came acquainted, I'll tell
    you in brief,   10
If you would but listen awhile;
For this very jest, among all the rest,
    I think it may cause you to smile.

ROBIN HOOD	For Robin Hood said to his jolly
[SINGLE VOICE]	bowmen,

°The refrain, which is a popular feature of ballads, should be recited after the first line of every stanza. Like many refrains, this one is nonsense—just like some sounds in popular songs today.

"Pray tarry you here in this grove; 15
And see that you all observe well my
    call,
  While through the forest I rove.

"We have had no sport for these
    fourteen long days,
  Therefore now abroad will I go;
Now should I be beat, and cannot
    retreat, 20
  My horn I will presently blow."

1ST CHORUS   Then did he shake hands with his
    merry men all,
  And bid them at present good-bye;
Then, as near the brook his journey
    he took,
  A stranger he chanced to espy. 25

They happened to meet on a long
    narrow bridge,
  And neither of them would give way;
Quoth bold Robin Hood, and sturdily
    stood,
ROBIN HOOD   "I'll shew you right Nottingham
    play."

1ST CHORUS   With that from his quiver an arrow he
    drew, 30
  A broad arrow with a goosewing.
LITTLE JOHN   The stranger replied, "I'll liquor thy
    hide,
  If thou offerst to touch the string."

ROBIN HOOD   Quoth bold Robin Hood, "Thou dost
         prate like an ass,
           For were I to bend but my bow,   35
         I could send a dart quite through thy
          proud heart,
           Before thou couldst strike me one
            blow."

LITTLE JOHN   "Thou talkst like a coward," the
         stranger replied;
          "Well armed with a long bow you
          stand,
         To shoot at my breast, while I, I protest, 40
          Have nought but a staff in my hand."

ROBIN HOOD   "The name of a coward," quoth Robin,
         "I scorn,
          Wherefore my long bow I'll lay by,
        And now, for thy sake, a staff will I take,
          The truth of thy manhood to try."   45

1ST CHORUS   Then Robin Hood stept to a thicket of
         trees,
          And chose him a staff of ground oak;
        Now this being done, away he did run
          To the stranger, and merrily spoke:

ROBIN HOOD   "Lo! see my staff is lusty and tough,   50
          Now here on the bridge we will play;
        Whoever falls in, the other shall win
          The battle, and so we'll away."

LITTLE JOHN   "With all my whole heart," the stranger
         replied,

	"I scorn in the least to give out";	
1ST CHORUS	This said, they fell to 't without more	
	dispute,	55
	And their staffs they did flourish	
	about.	
	At first Robin he gave the stranger a	
	bang,	
	So hard that he made his bones ring:	
LITTLE JOHN	The stranger he said, "This must be	
	repaid,	60
	I'll give you as good as you bring.	
	"So long as I am able to handle a staff,	
	To die in your debt, friend, I scorn."	
1ST CHORUS	Then to it each goes, and followed their	
	blows,	
	As if they'd been threshing of corn.	65

The stranger gave Robin a crack on the
    crown,
    Which caused the blood to appear;
Then Robin, enraged, more fiercely
    engaged,
    And followed his blows more severe.

So thick and so fast did he lay it on
    him,   70
    With a passionate fury and ire;
At every stroke he made him to smoke,
    As if he had been all on fire.

O then into fury the stranger he grew,
    And gave him a damnable look,   75

And with it a blow that laid him full low,
And tumbled him into the brook.

LITTLE JOHN   "I prithee, good fellow, where art thou
    now?"
The stranger, in laughter, he cried.
ROBIN HOOD   Quoth bold Robin Hood, "Good faith,
    in the flood,   80
  And floating along with the tide.

"I needs must acknowledge thou art a
    brave soul,
  With thee I'll no longer contend;
For needs must I say, thou hast got the
    day,
  Our battle shall be at an end."   85

1ST CHORUS   Then unto the bank he did presently
    wade,
  And pulled himself out by a thorn;
Which done, at the last he blowed a loud
    blast
  Straightway on his fine bugle horn:

The echo of which through the valleys
    did fly,   90
  At which his stout bowmen
    appeared,
All clothed in green, most gay to be seen,
  So up to their master they steered.

WILL STUTLY   "O, what's the matter?" quoth William
    Stutly,
"Good master you are wet to the skin."   95

ROBIN HOOD   "No matter," quoth he, "the lad which
you see
     In fighting hath tumbled me in."

3RD CHORUS   "He shall not go scot free," the others
replied.

1ST CHORUS   So straight they were seizing him
there,
     To duck him likewise: but Robin Hood
cries,   100

ROBIN HOOD   "He is a stout fellow; forbear.

"There's no one shall wrong thee, friend,
be not afraid;
     These bowmen upon me do wait;
There's three score and nine; if thou wilt
be mine,
     Thou shalt have my livery straight,   105

"And other accoutrements fit for a man.
     Speak up, jolly blade, never fear;
I'll teach you also the use of the bow,
     To shoot at the fat fallow deer."

LITTLE JOHN   "O, here is my hand," the stranger
replied,   110
     "I'll serve you with all my whole
heart;
My name is John Little, a man of good
mettle;
     Ne'er doubt me, for I'll play my part."

WILL STUTLY   "His name shall be altered," quoth
William Stutly,

"And I will his godfather be;   115
Prepare then a feast, and none of the
    least
For we will be merry," quoth he.

1ST CHORUS   They presently fetched him a brace of fat
    does,
    With humming strong liquor
        likewise;
They loved what was good, so in the
    green wood,   120
    This pretty sweet babe they baptize.

He was, I must tell you, but seven foot
    high,
    And, may be, an ell in the waist;
A sweet pretty lad; much feasting they
    had;
    Bold Robin the christening graced,   125

With all his bowmen, which stood in a
    ring,
    And were of the Nottingham breed;
Brave Stutly came then, with seven
    yeomen,
    And did in this manner proceed:

WILL STUTLY   "This infant was called John Little,"
    quoth he;   130
    "Which name shall be changed
        anon;
The words we'll transpose; so wherever
    he goes,
    His name shall be called Little John."

1ST CHORUS   They all with a shout made the elements
                  ring;
              So soon as the office was o'er,   135
              To feasting they went, with true
                  merriment,
              And tippled strong liquor gillore.

Jabberwocky

Lewis Carroll

CHORUS
'Twas brillig, and the slithy toves
    Did gyre and gimble in the wabe;
All mimsy were the borogoves,
    And the mome raths outgrabe.

FATHER
"Beware the Jabberwock, my son!   5
    The jaws that bite, the claws that
        catch!
Beware the Jubjub bird, and shun
    The frumious Bandersnatch!"

NARRATOR 1
He took his vorpal sword in hand;
    Long time the manxome foe he
        sought—   10
So rested he by the Tumtum tree,
    And stood awhile in thought.

NARRATOR 2
And, as in uffish thought he stood,
    The Jabberwock, with eyes of flame,
Came whiffling through the tulgey
        wood,   15
    And burbled as it came!

NARRATOR 3
One, two! One, two! And through and
        through
The vorpal blade went snicker-snack!

	He left it dead, and with its head	
	He went galumphing back.	20

FATHER   "And hast thou slain the Jabberwock?
          Come to my arms, my beamish boy!
          O frabjous day! Callooh! Callay!"
          He chortled in his joy.

CHORUS   'Twas brillig, and the slithy toves   25
          Did gyre and gimble in the wabe;
          All mimsy were the borogoves,
          And the mome raths outgrabe.

To read about Lewis Carroll, see the biographical sketch on page 121.

Brian's Song
William Blinn

Reading a Teleplay

In a **screenplay** (a script for a movie) or a **teleplay** (a script for TV) the camera directions are very important. Camera directions help you imagine what you would see on the screen. Like many teleplays, *Brian's Song* uses a **narrator,** or unseen speaker, to comment on the action.

Study this list of terms so that you can recognize and understand them as you read *Brian's Song:*

Voice-over: the voice of a character who is off camera or who is on camera but not shown to be speaking.

Fade In: The picture slowly appears on the screen.

Fade Out: The picture slowly disappears from the screen.

Exterior: outdoors.

Interior: indoors.

Beat: pause.

Long shot: a view from a distance.

Tight on; close shot: a close-up camera shot.

Full shot: a camera shot showing a complete view of the character(s) or scene.

Pan: short for *panorama;* the camera swings slowly from one side of the set to the other.

Hard cut to: shift abruptly to (a different scene).

Angle on or to: position the camera on (a character or scene).

Zoom: move in quickly for a close view or away for a distant view.

Freeze frame; hold: remain focused on one image for a few seconds.

Characters

NARRATOR: *voice that comments on the action*

BRIAN PICCOLO, GALE SAYERS: *running backs for the Chicago Bears*

GEORGE HALAS: *coach of the Bears*

J. C. CAROLINE, ABE GIBRON, ED MCCASKEY: *assistant coaches of the Bears*

ATKINS, EVEY, O'BRADOVICH: *players for the Bears*

REPORTERS

LINDA SAYERS: *Gale's wife*

JOY PICCOLO: *Brian's wife*

SPEAKER: *at an awards ceremony*

JACK CONCANNON: *quarterback of the Bears*

ANNOUNCER: *radio sportscaster*

DR. FOX: *who treats Gale*

NURSES

HOTEL OFFICIAL

PLAYER: *Gale's new roommate*

MR. EBERLE: *hospital official*

DOCTOR: *who gives Brian anesthesia*

M.C.: *master of ceremonies*

Part One

Fade In:

Exterior—Rolling countryside—Day (helicopter shot)
The terrain is farmland, flat, tranquil, soothing in its simplic-
ity. As our view gets closer to the ground, we start to hear the
Narrator's voice.

NARRATOR *(voice-over).* This is a story about two men, one
named Gale Sayers, the other Brian Piccolo. They came
from different parts of the country. They competed for the
same job. One was white; the other black. One liked to
talk; the other was as shy as a three-year-old. Our story's
about how they came to know each other, fight each
other, and help each other. . . .
   (beat)
Ernest Hemingway said that every true story ends in
death. Well, this *is* a true story.

As the helicopter continues its descent, we now find ourselves
following a cab down a two-lane asphalt road. We follow the cab
as we roll opening credits.

Direct cut to:

Exterior—Campus-type area—Day—On sign
Reading "Training Camp of the Chicago Bears," an NFL
insignia beneath the lettering. We pan off the sign, moving by a
number of red-brick buildings, the kind of ivied architecture
seen at any number of small universities in the Middle West.
Coming up the curving blacktopped drive is the cab.

Exterior—Practice field—Series of cuts
The Bears are going through the various routines and exercises.
Defensive linemen scuttling crablike back and forth as a coach
switches a ball from hand to hand. Men working on the blocking

sled, throwing their bulk against the padded metal arm. Players negotiating the rope framework, some alternating, crossing over, others hopping from square to square. Throughout these cuts, the sounds of men under strain, struggling for breath, grunting with effort as they bear down.

As we zoom toward the far end of the field, we see Gale Sayers standing by the driver's side of the cab, his suitcase next to him.

Sayers is in his early twenties, his handsome face normally enigmatic, guarded. He's dressed in slacks and sport coat, but even in this kind of "civilian" garb, it doesn't take a practiced eye to note the lean, hard compactness of a born athlete.

BRIAN *(voice-over).* Heads up! Look out!

Gale looks toward the sound of the voice just in time to react to the football hurtling down toward him. He gets a hand up and slaps it away, over the cab. Gale walks across to the other side of the road to get the football and throws it to the young man now approaching him. He's wearing a Bears sweat shirt, workout shorts, football cleats. This is Brian Piccolo—early twenties, with a smile that comes easily and nicely. He takes life and people as he finds them, and he generally finds them worthwhile, enjoyable, and a little funny. The face is strong and handsome. Gale throws the ball back across the road to him.

GALE. Here you go.
BRIAN. Thanks.

Brian heaves the ball back to the practice area offstage, though he makes no move to return there himself. Gale is a little ill at ease as Brian just stands there looking at him with a half smile.

BRIAN. You're Gale Sayers.
GALE. Yeah.
BRIAN. I'm Brian Piccolo. We met at the All-America game last June in Buffalo.

Brian has extended his hand, but Gale is holding his suitcase. A short beat as Gale switches hands, but by the time it's done, Brian has taken back his hand, and there's a moment of stuttering reactions. Finally, they shake hands. Gale's head is down, face guarded.

GALE. Sorry I didn't remember, but I'm not very good at that kind of stuff.

Piccolo's smile is a nice one.

BRIAN *(a quiet put-on)*. Golly, that's okay. I can see why you might forget, but I sure couldn't. No way. That was a heckuva talk we had, man. I mean, I walked up and said: "I'm Brian Piccolo. I hear we'll both be playing for the Bears." And you said—I'll never forget it—you said: "Uh-huh." Just like that. "Uh-huh." And whenever I'm feeling depressed or low, why, I think about that advice. Lot of guys wouldn't have taken the time to talk to me like that, but not you. "Uh-huh," you said. Just like that. Right out.

Brian grins. Gale does not. His expression is neutral. A short beat.

GALE. Where do I go to check in?

Piccolo's smile goes. The total lack of reaction from Gale is puzzling. He nods toward one of the buildings offstage.

BRIAN. That building over there. That's where Halas is.
GALE. Thanks.

The word comes in a characteristic flat tone. Gale moves off for the building. Brian stands there a moment, looking after him thoughtfully.

BRIAN. Hey . . .

Gale stops, looking back.

GALE. What?

BRIAN. You ever met Halas before?

GALE. Talked to him on the phone a couple times. That's all.

Brian's manner is calm, pleasant, helpful.

BRIAN. Well, look, let me give you a little hint. He's a good guy and all, but he's deaf in his left ear and he's too vain to admit it. So stay on his right-hand side, or he won't hear a word you say.

(*beat*)

GALE. Uh—okay. Thanks.

BRIAN. Rookies have to stick together, man.

With a wave of his hand, Brian starts off, moving at an easy lope back onto the practice field. Sayers stands there, watching Brian, not knowing precisely what to make of him. After a moment, he turns and starts for the building pointed out by Piccolo.

Direct cut to:

Interior—Bears' main office corridor—Full shot

Gale comes in looking about uneasily, then heads for the end of the corridor. He stops in front of a door with a nameplate reading "Coach George Halas," wipes his sweating palms on his trouser legs, then knocks on the door.

HALAS (*impatiently, offstage*). Yeah. Come in.

Gale stands motionless for a second, gathering his forces, then opens the door and steps inside.

Interior—Halas's office—Full shot

As Gale comes into the office, he starts to speak, but his voice is only a dry croak. The office is in a state of organized chaos. Cardboard filing boxes, cartons of books, and papers. Reels of film and, standing behind an ancient desk, a large man of some years, some strength, and much power: Halas. He holds a framed picture, hammer, and nails. He looks at the young man standing in the doorway.

HALAS. I'm George Halas.

GALE. I know. *(Quickly)* I mean, everyone knows who you are. I'm Gale Sayers.

HALAS. Come on in, Gale. You can give me a hand hanging this thing. My good luck picture. First professional team I ever played on. The Decatur Staleys in 1920.

Gale steps in, closing the door, still awed and afraid. Halas moves to an empty place on the wall, his back to Gale.

HALAS. How's your leg? I read where it was hurt.

GALE. It's fine. Hundred percent.

HALAS. How about your head?

GALE. My head? Nothin' wrong with my head.

HALAS. Good. Because being in the All-Star game puts you three weeks behind everybody else. New terminology, new plays to learn. Won't be easy.

(beat)

GALE. NFL ain't supposed to be easy.

A smile and look from Halas. He nods.

HALAS. Right. Give me a hand.

Gale moves behind the desk, where Halas is holding the picture up against the wall. Halas starts hammering a nail.

HALAS. About all I can promise you is a fair shot at running back. But you're going to have a lot of company. Jon Arnett, Ralph Kurek, Brian Piccolo . . . going to be very crowded out there.

Gale looks at Halas for a second, realizing he's on the man's left side, recalling the advice given him by Brian earlier. He rumbas around behind and then to the other side of the Coach.

GALE. Well, a fair shot is all I want. Can't ask for more than that.

Halas notes Gale's shift with a puzzled look, then drives the nail home. He turns back to the desk, once more placing Gale on his left side.

HALAS. We plan to use our backs a good deal as receivers this year. You do much pass catching when you were in college?

He looks back to where Gale was, only to find that Gale has crossed behind him.

GALE. Well, yes sir, I did, but it was usually safety-valve stuff. Once in a while we'd screen.

Halas moves to one of the filing cabinets nearby.

HALAS. Well, I generally prefer to get a back into the pattern, unless the other team has a tendency to blitz. That's another thing you'll have to get used to, checking out the linebackers, make sure they aren't coming.

Halas looks back to Gale, but once again, he's the man who isn't there. Gale has managed to cross behind him again, squeezing in between Halas and the wall, struggling to make the move seem casual.

GALE. Yes sir, I know . . .

Halas starts back to the desk, once again forcing Gale to do an end around.

GALE. . . . and, especially on teams like the Cardinals, I guess . . .

HALAS (*exasperated*). Sayers—what's the matter with you?

GALE. I—I don't know what you mean . . .

HALAS. I know you've got moves, but you don't have to

show them to me now! You're hopping around here like a pauper in a pay toilet!

GALE (*sputtering*). Well, I—I was just trying to stay on the side with your good ear . . .

HALAS. Good ear? What are you talking about, good ear?

GALE. Well, Brian Piccolo told me that—he said—uh—he—uh . . .

Halas waits for the sentence to end, but it's not going to. For the realization is slowly dawning on Gale that he has been had. Gale struggles to manufacture a smile as Halas stares at him.

Direct cut to:

Interior—Dining hall—Night—Angle on steam table
The table is piled with food being assaulted by a number of large men, who ladle on portions that would choke a garbage disposal. At a centrally placed table, we can see Halas, his coaches, and key players.

Closer angle—Coaches' table
Seated on one side of Halas is Ed McCaskey, a handsome man in his early fifties. On the other side is Abe Gibron, a man who is all football. One man at the table is standing. This is J. C. Caroline, a man in his late twenties, tall and lean, built for speed. He has a packet of three-by-five index cards he consults as he speaks.

CAROLINE. Some of you guys who pulled in today haven't had a chance to hear what's going to be expected of you, so pipe down for a little bit, let me talk.

Angle on Gale
He is seated at one of the rear tables, exchanging "pass-the-salt" conversations with the other men nearby, all of whom are black. The man next to Gale finishes his plate and vacates the chair as Caroline continues to speak offstage. Brian Piccolo approaches and starts to unload his tray in the place next to Gale. Gale tries to hide his displeasure.

CAROLINE *(droning offstage)*. You new guys are going to be given a playbook tomorrow. It's like the Bible, except the Gideons don't replace it for free. Neither do the Bears. Lose the playbook and the fine is five hundred dollars. No exceptions, no appeal. Five-double-o. Second thing is curfew. You don't like it; I don't like it. Well, that's just tough sleddin', because that fine is ten bucks for every fifteen minutes and there's no appeal from that either. Now—for talking in team meeting . . .

Caroline becomes aware of Gale and Brian speaking offstage.

BRIAN. Sayers, we can't go on meeting like this—my wife's getting suspicious.
GALE. Buzz off. I'm trying to listen to the Man.
BRIAN. No need, no need. I've been through this lecture twice already. If you lose the playbook, a fine of five big ones. Lose the playbook a second time, and they cut off your foot and feed it to the defensive platoon.
GALE. Just cool it, would you, please?
BRIAN. Just trying to be helpful.
GALE. Yes—like you "helped" me with Halas. Well, I don't need your kind of . . .
CAROLINE *(loudly offstage)*. Mister Sayers!

Wider angle
J. C. Caroline fixes Gale with the look that's chilled any number of feckless flankers. Every eye in the room is on Gale, and most are relishing his pained reaction.

CAROLINE *(continuing)*. I was mentioning the fine for talking in a team meeting. Did you happen to hear me?
GALE. No, I did not.
CAROLINE. The fine is twenty-five dollars, Mr. Sayers. And it's just been levied on you, *dig?*
GALE *(seething)*. Yeah.

Piccolo stares straight ahead, lips trembling as he tries to mask the laughter building up within him.

BRIAN *(sotto).* Sorry, man . . .

Gale glares at him, homicide in mind. Slow homicide.
Caroline gets to his feet, tapping the water glass for attention.

CAROLINE. It's been brought to my attention that unless Sayers was saying his beads it might be fair if Mr. Piccolo was to give us a little song. Say—a fight song. Wake Forest, wasn't it, Mr. Piccolo?

Angle to Brian and Gale
Gale's look acknowledges that there may be some justice in this old world after all. To his surprise, however, the singing troubles Brian not at all. He smiles, rising, and when he sees the surprise on Gale's face, leans over to whisper.

BRIAN. Can't let it get to you, man—it's all a question of *style.* Style, I say . . .

He is up on the chair, launching into the Wake Forest fight song, giving it a rousing tempo and booming volume. Brian thrives on this kind of thing. Gale's eye falls on something offstage in the direction of Brian's plate.

Gale's point of view—The plate
Shot is centered on two mammoth dollops of mashed potatoes swimming in rich brown gravy.

Angle on Gale
He takes a spoon and fork, glancing up to make sure Brian is still concentrating on the song, then moves to transfer the potatoes to the seat of Brian's chair.
As he finishes the song, Brian waves a cordial hand to those clapping, then hops down lightly and sits—without looking.

Gale just sits there, looking at Brian, enjoying the rush of expressions that go rolling across his face. Disbelief. Dread. Realization. A look to the absent mashed potatoes on his plate. Acceptance. By the time he slowly swings his look over to Gale, Gale is just getting to his feet, face composed. Before he goes, however, he reminds Brian.

GALE. It's all a question of style—style, I say . . .

He moves off, camera closing on Piccolo. He turns squishily, watching Gale saunter off. He can't quite work up a smile, but neither can he get to a point of being very angry about it. He can take it as well as hand it out, it seems.

Direct cut to:

Exterior—Practice field—Day—Tight on Gibron

Abe Gibron is an assistant coach possessed of a voice that could shatter glass. When we pull back, we will see that Gibron is presently riding herd on a number of offensive backs, Sayers and Piccolo in the forefront, as they lower their heads and dig against the resistance of the harness looped about their shoulders and fastened to a stone wall. Gibron will not be happy until one of the men pulls down the wall.

GIBRON. Dig! Dig! Dig! Come on! What's wrong with you? You're not trying! You're not trying! You make me sick! Dig—dig—dig!

Hard cut to:

Exterior—Practice field—Day—Full shot

Fifty men hit the dirt, then are up on their feet, running in place.

GIBRON. Mark! Set! Go!

Sayers and Piccolo come out of a sprinter's crouch, taking each other on in wind sprints, their faces locked with drive and desire.

Angle to the forty-yard line

Halas and a number of other coaches are standing. Gale tears across the line a full stride ahead of the others. Stopwatches are held out for Halas's perusal. He notes the results and is pleased.

Angle on Gale and Brian

They draw up, both sagging, leaning forward, hands on knees as they try to pull more air in. This may be the tenth wind sprint they've run today. Between gasps of breath:

BRIAN. Well—I think it's working.

GALE. What's working?

BRIAN. I'm getting you overconfident.

Hard cut to:

Interior—Team meeting room—Day—On blackboard

A play is diagramed on the blackboard, the area covered with circles and X's, dotted lines, and arrows. Halas is the man with the chalk. No need to hear what he's saying—his look and the manner in which he raps the chalk against the slate get the message across.

Angle on Sayers and Piccolo

They are seated near the front with the rest of the players, all of whom are studying the board as if their lives depended on it. Which, in one sense, it does. The look of exhaustion is shared by all as they listen and frantically scribble notes.

Direct cut to:

Exterior—Practice field—Day—Full shot

The offense and defense take measure of one another. They line up, the ball is snapped. There is a brief flurry of motion, then the quarterback is downed by a large man from the defensive unit. As they all untangle themselves to the accompaniment of the whistles, Brian gets up and finds himself being glared at by Abe Gibron.

GIBRON. Pic! You bonehead! That was a fake draw, screen

right! What's your assignment on a fake draw, screen right?

BRIAN. My assignment on a fake draw, screen right, is to pick up the linebacker, if he's coming, unless the linebacker is Dick Butkus. Then I simply notify the quarterback and send for a priest.

Laughter from the others on this, which only further enrages Gibron.

Angle on Gale
He is smiling broadly at Piccolo's reply—smiling, perhaps, in spite of himself.

GIBRON *(offstage).* Come on, you guys, don't! You just encourage him, that's all! Knock it off!

Direct cut to:
Exterior—Practice field—Night—Full shot
Gale moves along the walk bordering the practice area, dressed in casual sports clothes, an after-dinner stroll. He nears us, then stops, looking offstage, expression puzzled.

His point of view—On Brian
In the middle of the empty practice field, he falls into a three-point stance, counts off a whispered series of signals, then breaks to his right. Just as he's about to turn upfield, he brakes sharply and cocks his arm, letting an imaginary pass go. Apparently, the imaginary receiver caught the ball, because Piccolo's expression is pleased as he turns back—and sees Gale watching his pantomime. He shrugs.

BRIAN. I'm dynamite until there's someone playing against me.

Another angle
Gale moves to him, still a little puzzled.

BRIAN. Practicing the halfback option. I'm not too good at it, and it looks as if they want to use it a lot.
GALE (*politely*). Oh, you'll get the hang of it.

Brian smiles.

BRIAN. Wish I was as sure of that as you are. Tell you the truth, Sayers—I envy you.
GALE. How come?
BRIAN. Because they've got a lot of money tied up in you. They can't cut you.

Gale just looks at him for a second, then turns abruptly and starts off.

BRIAN (*simply*). And you're too good to get cut, bonus or no bonus.

Gale stops, turns back slowly.
    (*beat*)

BRIAN. And I'm too good, too, but I'm not sure I've proved that to the Old Man yet.

Gale is thrown off stride mentally. Piccolo's easy directness takes some getting used to. Brian views him with a small smile.

BRIAN. Sayers—I am bending over backwards to get through that turtle shell of yours. Can't you at least say thank you or something?
GALE. Well—I don't do things like you do—telling jokes and all that kind of—you know—I—I'm more of a . . . (*Considers*) Thanks.

A quick nod, then Gale turns and heads back in the direction of the dormitory. Piccolo smiles, taking even this small break-through as some kind of progress. He gets to his feet and is about to go through the halfback option once more.

GALE. Hey, Piccolo?
BRIAN. Yeah?
GALE. Try it going to your left. They don't look for a right-handed guy to throw going to his left.

Brian nods, smiling as their eyes meet; Gale's look still a guarded one.
    (beat)

BRIAN. Thanks.

Gale shrugs, glances down.

GALE. Well, like you said—us rookies got to stick together.

Hard cut to:
Interior—Hallway outside Halas's office—Day—On door
Gale raps on the door several times.

HALAS *(offstage)*. Come on in, Gale.

Gale opens the door and steps in, camera following to reveal Halas behind the desk, Ed McCaskey seated nearby, and J. C. Caroline doodling on the blackboard. Gale views the three with a mixture of fear and curiosity.

HALAS. You know Ed McCaskey, don't you, Gale? And J.C.?

Affirmative ad-libs come from Gale and the other two men. Gale takes the chair that has obviously been left vacant for him. Halas nods toward a pitcher of iced tea.

HALAS. Want some iced tea?
GALE. Uh, yeah. Please.

Halas pours him a glass, the cubes tinkling. Gale fidgets. Halas hands him the glass.

HALAS. Tell you what we wanted to talk to you about,

Gale . . . See, I'm an old-timer in a lot of ways . . . (*A look to Caroline and McCaskey*) At least that's what people keep telling me—but I don't think it's all that uncommon for a man my age to get used to the way things are—to be comfortable with things. You understand what I'm saying?

GALE (*baffled*). I guess so. . . .

HALAS. Well, what it comes down to is that J.C. here had a notion and he talked to Ed about it, and Ed thinks it's a good idea—and I guess maybe it's time for some changes around here. You follow me?

GALE. You want me to play flanker, not running back.

The other three exchange a smile at this.

MCCASKEY. Not that simple, Gale. J.C.'s point—and one I agree with—is that it's 1965 and it's time the Bears roomed together by position—without any regard to race.

CAROLINE. We'd like you and Brian Piccolo to room together.

Gale smiles with relief.

GALE. Is that all? Is that what this is about?

CAROLINE. Is that *all*?

GALE. Yeah. You had me worried. I thought it was something really . . .

Tight on Caroline
His index finger shoots out, pinning Gale to the chair.

CAROLINE. Sayers—this *is* something, really. This is a white man and a black man rooming together on a team where that's never been done before. You're going to be called a Tom by some blacks and uppity by some whites. And when we go on the road, we'll be going to Atlanta and Dallas and Houston and Miami—and don't think it's going to get any better in Los Angeles and Detroit and Chicago, and every other town we play in, 'cause it *won't*.

(beat)
You're going to rock the boat, Sayers—and there's plenty
of people around who are already seasick.

*A beat, as Caroline holds Gale's gaze, then straightens up.
Halas has a small smile on his face.*

HALAS. Have a glass of iced tea, J.C.

Halas leans forward.

HALAS. What J.C. is saying is that there may be pressures,
Gale. Severe ones. *(Simply)* Now! What do *you* say?

*Gale takes a breath, looking beyond the three men, giving the
question the introspection it deserves.*

Direct cut to:

Interior—Dormitory hallway—Night—On Brian
*Brian comes down the hallway, wearing a windbreaker and
casual slacks. Offstage we can hear the sound of muted rock
music. Brian's face is set, dour and depressed. He stops in front
of one of the doors, pulls a key out of his pocket, then registers:
That music is coming from his room. He looks down at the
space between the door and the floor. There's light peeping out
from within the room. Puzzled, he puts the key in the lock and
opens the door cautiously.*

Interior—The room
*A picture is thumbtacked to the bulletin board, of Joy Piccolo
and a baby girl. We pan over to reveal another picture tacked up
on the bulletin board next to Joy's. The second picture is of
Linda Sayers. We pan down from this picture to find Gale
sprawled out on the bed, the radio blaring by his side. He
reaches out and turns off the radio.*

GALE. Hi. We're rooming together.
BRIAN. Says who?
GALE. Who else?

BRIAN (*sourly*). Terrific. Sort of a shame he couldn't ask me how I felt about it, isn't it?

GALE (*warily*). Look, if you want me out . . .

BRIAN. No, stay, I don't want you out. I'm just steamed at the Old Man for not putting me in the scrimmage this afternoon.

(*beat*)

Is that your wife?

GALE. Yeah.

BRIAN. She's pretty.

GALE. So's yours. And the little girl.

BRIAN (*still down*). Thanks. I'm supposed to call her tonight—tell her how I'm doing. Be the shortest phone call in history.

GALE. Maybe not.

When Piccolo looks over at him, Gale smiles.

GALE. Pic—they wouldn't assign us to room together unless we *both* made the team.

Brian looks over at Gale and it hits him. He moves to Gale, pulling him off the bed and shoving him toward the door.

BRIAN. Come on! We've got to call our wives!

GALE. I already called Linda, right after . . .

BRIAN. That was just practice! This is for real! Come on!

And the two of them go tumbling out into the corridor.

Full shot—The corridor

Atkins, O'Bradovich, and Evey are standing a few feet away— huge men, arms like hams, necks like tree stumps. Their expressions are insolent, challenging, but not cruel. Each of them has a coffee can in hand. Each container holds a sticky-looking, evil-smelling conglomeration of honey, cereal, sand, catsup, and whatever they could lay their hands on. They move in unison toward Brian and Gale.

ATKINS. Congratulations on making the team, gentlemen. Well done.

EVEY. As you know, Coach Halas frowns on the hazing of new men.

O'BRADOVICH. But now that you've made the team—it's really like—you're one of us.

All three have wooden spoons in the ooze, lifting the dripping, brown gunk for all to see. In a second, they're all tearing down the hall. Gale and Brian are bent low, the three pursuers bellowing with the thrill of the hunt. The last words echo in the corridor as all the doors are opened and men stick their heads out to see which rookies are getting it now.

ATKINS (*yelling*). Welcome to the Chicago Bears!

Interior—Bears' locker room—Day—Full shot
Gale is in front of his locker, just pulling off his jersey, which is muddy and torn. Two reporters are on each side of him. Piccolo, whose uniform looks as if he stepped out of a catalog, is seated in front of his locker, taking it all in with a certain objective humor. Gale, typically, is ill at ease in this kind of situation.

REPORTER #1. Is playing in the NFL easier than you thought it would be?

GALE. Only played one game. Not exactly an expert.

REPORTER #2. But you didn't look as if you were having too much trouble out there.

GALE. The blocks were there.

BRIAN. Sure is different from the way you were talking last night, Gale. (*To reporters*) He calls the offensive line the "seven blocks of Silly Putty."

GALE. Pic——

REPORTER #1. You're Brian Piccolo?

BRIAN. P—I—C—C—O—L—O, yes.

Direct cut to:
NFL footage
A long run from scrimmage by Sayers.

BRIAN *(voice-over)*. Gale, when you run, do you think about what you're doing, or do you just do it?
GALE *(voice-over)*. I just do it.
BRIAN *(voice-over)*. Well, start thinking about it, will you? I want to play, too.

Direct cut to:
Interior—Pizza parlor—Night—Full shot
Grouped about one of the tables are Gale, Brian, and their wives, Joy Piccolo and Linda Sayers. They're at ease with one another, just now finishing off a casual, enjoyable evening on the town. They are listening to one of Brian's stories. He's telling it well, laughing as he does so, and it's a catching kind of thing for the women. Gale, being Gale, allows himself a small smile, but little beyond that.

BRIAN. Now—picture this—Concannon calls a trap, see. . . . *(To Linda and Joy)* You know what a trap is?
LINDA *(unsure)*. I think so, but—maybe . . .
BRIAN. Well—uh—all the linemen go one way and hopefully the defense guys go that way, too. If they do, there's a big hole, see? If they don't—bad news. Anyway—Concannon calls a trap up the middle, Gale carrying the ball. It works like they draw it on the blackboard. Forty-three yards. Beautiful. So, Halas sees Gale's winded; he tells me to go in. So, I go in; Gale comes out. We get in the huddle—Concannon decides he's going to get foxy. He calls the *same* play. The very same play. Last thing they'll be looking for, he says. Now—the trap play is also called the "sucker play" because the defense really looks bad when it works—and defenses don't like to look bad—makes 'em surly.

Joy, who's heard this story a hundred times already, has started to laugh, anticipating Brian's big finish.

BRIAN. So—we come out of the huddle—ball's snapped—all our linemen go one way—and it's like I'm looking at a team portrait of the Los Angeles Rams—Hello, Deacon . . . Merlin, how's the family . . . Rosey . . .

Laughter from them all, ad-libs between the girls. Gale's smile has broadened now and Brian's just having a fine old time.

BRIAN. I mean—I was afraid to get up. I figured not everything was going to come with me. . . .
JOY *(nicely).* You never saw anyone so black and blue.
GALE. Yeah—it was like rooming with a black player again.

Gale grins—and the other three gape, looking at him with expressions of shock. His smile turns uneasy, bewildered. He checks to make sure there's no anchovy hanging off his chin.

LINDA. Gale—you told a *joke.*
BRIAN. Joy—did you hear it? The great Stone Face from Kansas told a joke!

Brian turns to the other patrons, cupping his hands about his mouth.

BRIAN *(yelling).* Chicago! There's hope for us all! Sayers speaks!
GALE. Aw, come *on*, Pic. . . .

But Gale's smiling, pleased with himself if the truth were known, as is Linda Sayers. The camera holds on them.

Direct cut to:
NFL footage of a Sayers run—Slow motion
This footage should be the most impressive of all, selling the power and grace of Sayers's ability.

BRIAN (*voice-over*). Magic—I think I'm going to write you a speech.

GALE (*voice-over*). What kind of speech?

BRIAN (*voice-over*). Acceptance speech for "Rookie of the Year." You can't miss.

GALE (*voice-over*). And I got to give a speech? You're putting me on!

Direct cut to:

Interior—Banquet dais—Night—Tight spot

Offstage the sound of a speaker drones on. Gale, Linda, Brian, and Joy are on the dais—the men in tuxedos, the women in formal gowns. Brian has a crumpled piece of paper in his hand. He leans into Gale, speaking in an urgent whisper.

BRIAN. From the top. One more time.

GALE (*harried, by rote*). I'd like to thank you all for this honor, though it's really not right to give it to one man. Football is a—team sport, and I . . .

SPEAKER (*offstage*). Gale Sayers!

A spotlight floods the area and we hear offstage applause. Gale is urged to his feet by Brian and Linda. He moves toward the speaker's platform, petrified. All we can see is Gale; the harsh pinpoint of the carbon arc is centered on him with no residual spillage. He looks at the trophy for a second.

GALE (*trembling*). I'd—I'd like to thank you all for this honor, though it's really not right . . .

He stops. He stops because he can't think of the next word. It's gone. Nothing there. Joy and Linda agonize in the silence, trying to pray more words out of Gale. Brian can't believe it. He starts to slowly tear the speech up, shaking his head, grinning. Gale's mouth is like Death Valley.

GALE. Thank you.

Brian tosses the pieces of paper in the air, like confetti, smiling.

BRIAN. Who'd believe it—who'd ever believe it. . . .

Direct cut to:

Exterior—Sayers's house—Night

BRIAN. Hey, Gale?
Gale holds on the porch. Linda waves a hand toward the car, her words intended for Gale.
LINDA. Too cold out here. I'll warm your side of the bed.

She moves into the house as Brian gets out of the car and trots to Gale, both men with shoulders hunched against the cold. Brian moves to him.

GALE. What do you want, man? It's freezing out here!
BRIAN. Something I've got to tell you.
GALE. What is it?

Gale notes an edge to Brian's voice, an undercurrent of reluctance, shyness. Brian looks him directly in the eye.

BRIAN. Joy and I had a long talk last night—about whether or not I should ask to be traded. We decided that I wouldn't ask. I like the guys on the team; I like the town.
  (beat)
What I *don't* like is playing second string.
GALE *(quietly)*. I don't blame you.
BRIAN. Now—*maybe* I've got a shot at fullback. But I don't think Halas thinks I'm big enough. He'll probably go with Ralph Kurek. The other spot is yours—and that's the job I'm gunning for, Gale.

Gale starts to reply, but Brian silences him with a gesture.

BRIAN. Let me get it said.
  (beat)
I'm a better blocker than you are and I'm as good a

receiver. And if I can't break away for sixty, I can still get
ten sixes, and it adds up the same way. I'm going to come
into camp next year in the best shape ever, and I think
I've got a realistic chance to blow you out of the lineup.
. . . And that's just what I'm going to try to do.

GALE. I understand, man—that's your job.

BRIAN. Yeah—but I don't like to do "a job" on a friend.

GALE (small smile). Don't worry; you won't.

*There's no anger between them, just resolve. After a beat, there
is a light tap on the car horn. Brian looks at the trophy: He
touches it lightly.*

BRIAN (as Bogart). It's a Maltese Falcon, kid—get this
inside—and the free world is safe.

*With that, Brian moves back to the car, camera holding on Gale
as he looks after his nutty friend, then down to the trophy. He
heads for the door.*

Direct cut to:

Interior—Halas's office—Day—On picture
*Another team picture is being tacked on the wall, the printing
identifying it as last year's Bears.*

Direct cut to:

Exterior—Practice field area—Day—Full shot
*Gale and Brian take positions in a line for wind sprints. Their
look to each other is friendly, but neither has precisely a fix on
what attitude is the working one. They speak as the line moves
forward. There are sounds of the other men yelling offstage.*

BRIAN. Hi. You just pull in?

GALE. Yeah. Would have been here this morning, but the
flight got fogged in in Detroit. You look in good shape.

BRIAN. I am. Worked hard this winter.

GIBRON (yelling offstage). Go!

Full shot
Brian takes off, arms pumping, but Gale is laughing at a joke Brian has just told. Brian is past the forty at least three seconds before Gale, grinning from ear to ear.

Gale draws up from his leisurely sprint. They haven't even kept the clock on his effort.

GALE. Mind if I try it again?
HALAS. Might be a good idea.

Gale starts to retrace his steps to the goal line, then draws up, looking back to Gibron and Halas.

GALE. What was Pic's time like?

Gibron consults the clipboard.

GIBRON. Must be out to get you. . . . He's about half a second faster this year than last.

Gale is not frightened, but properly impressed. He nods, taking it in. His expression denies his statement.

GALE. That's really terrific. . . .

Direct cut to:

Exterior—Practice field—Day—Full shot
A number of men dot the area going through calisthenics. We find Gale and Brian doing sit-ups, each being helped by another player who anchors their feet. They're facing in opposite directions so that, as they come up, they're looking at each other. The looks are not hostile, but there's very little "give" in each man's expression.

Direct cut to:

Exterior—Practice field—Day—Full shot
The offense and defense are performing the one-on-one drill. This time, it's Brian who's the offensive back and the move he puts on the defensive man is a beauty. As Brian tears out of

frame, we zoom in on Gale, impassive outwardly, but fully aware of what's going on.

Direct cut to:

Interior—Dormitory hallway—Night—Full shot
Gale and Brian come in from the outside, both wearing light jackets, Brian carrying a pizza box.

BRIAN. That's why you'll never cut it, Sayers—pizza has magical properties that give Italian guys strength and speed.

GALE. Yeah—a lot of great Italian running backs, all right.

BRIAN. Yeah. Jim Brownanelli. Lennie Moorelli. All those guys.

Angle to stairway
At the bottom is a bulletin board, where J. C. Caroline stands putting up a large sheet of paper. Brian moves by him, taking the stairs two at a time, and ad-libs a greeting, which is returned by J.C. Gale comes by.

GALE. What's that, J.C.?

CAROLINE. Starting lineups for the first exhibition.

Gale's eye moves toward the landing of the second floor. The shadow of Brian Piccolo can be seen. His head turns slowly, listening.

GALE. What's the backfield?

CAROLINE *(as he goes)*. Concannon, Ralph Kurek, and you.

If ever there were mixed emotions in a man, now is that time. Gale looks up.

His point of view—Brian's shadow
Sagging, head lowered. A long beat, then Brian takes a breath, straightens his shoulders and moves off, the shadow disappearing.

BRIAN *(offstage)*. Come on, Magic. . . . Pizza's getting cold.

Tight on Gale

He leans against the wall, disappointed and yet relieved at the same time. He looks toward the second-story landing once more, as we start to hear the growing roar of a large crowd, the unwavering roar of the hero seekers.

Direct cut to:

Exterior—Wrigley Field—Day—NFL footage

The stands are crowded with spectators. The day is damp and gray.

Angle to field—NFL footage

The Bears are playing the San Francisco 49ers.

Angle to Bears' bench

Gale's uniform, muddy and begrimed; Piccolo's with only a smudge or two. Halas and Gibron pace restlessly up and down the sidelines, yelling to the defensive unit, as are all the other players. Concannon is on the phones, listening intently.

Angle to field

The ball is snapped to 49er quarterback John Brodie and he backpedals, looking for a receiver going deep. Brodie gets the pass off, but it falls into the hands of a defensive back from the Chicago Bears.

Angle to bench

Every man is on his feet yelling. There is a flurry of activity—Gale is pulling on his helmet, receiving a pat from Brian. Concannon takes off the earphones and moves with the rest of the offensive team onto the field.

Angle to stands

LINDA. Go get 'em, Gale!! You can do it, honey!

Tight on Joy Piccolo

Happy at this turn of events but also painfully aware of something else, her eyes move from the field to the bench.

Her point of view—On Brian

With his back to the stands, helmet off, Number 41 paces rest-lessly back and forth along the sidelines. His attention is on the game, but the gaze drops a few times as inward moments take over.

Angle to Bears' huddle

CONCANNON. Yours, Gale. Twenty-eight toss. South. Line. On three. *Break!*

Full shot

The team comes out of the huddle, moving with precision into formation. Concannon looks over the defense and calls out the signals in a rhythmic cadence. The ball is snapped and Concannon pivots, the move coordinated with the pulling of the guards and Gale's instantaneous break to his left. The ball is tossed back to Gale. He takes the pitch-out and has the ball well in hand as he starts to look for an opening in the upfield area.

On Brian

He is at the water bucket, dipper poised as he stops to watch the play develop.

Back on Gale

Seemingly from nowhere, a San Francisco 49er uniform comes hurtling into frame and we freeze frame just before the shoulder of the player tears into Gale's knee. All crowd noises are killed. Only silence. The frame moves again now and we can see the awful impact. Freeze frame on this instant. The picture comes to life in short bursts as Gale crumples, knee landing at an angle to set one's teeth on edge, in jerky, grainy images.

On Brian

A freeze frame slowly moves forward half a step; he realizes what he's witnessing.

On Linda and Joy
They are very much afraid of what they're seeing. Linda's hand flies to her mouth.

Back on Gale
He hits the ground, one hand already going to the knee, the ball forgotten about. He tries to get to his feet, and the instant he puts any pressure on the knee, his head snaps back in reaction to the agony that assaults him. We freeze frame on Gale, every muscle contorted, and we hear the sound of a siren wailing, wailing, wailing.

Hard cut to:

Exterior—Sayers's home—Day—Full shot
The car, driven by Linda, pulls to a halt in the driveway. Gale opens the door and starts to get out. He's using two metal canes, the right leg swung out before him, stiff and unbending. His face is chiseled with tension and anger—cold, acid anger.

LINDA. Can I help?
GALE. No.

He makes his way slowly toward the front door, still not used to the canes, not yet using his body weight to help himself. Instead, it's a halting, unnatural motion—painful to execute, more painful for Linda to watch. She hurries past him to open the front door.

Interior—The living room—Day—Full shot
Gale comes in, no reaction to being home in his eyes. He moves to the first chair and sits.

LINDA. It's good to have you home, Gale.
GALE. Yeah. Good to be home.

But his eyes admit it was a reply made because it was the reply expected.

LINDA. Can I get you anything?

GALE. No. I'm fine.

LINDA. It's about lunch time. You want a sandwich or anything?

GALE. Not hungry; you go ahead, though.

LINDA. Are you sure?

GALE (*with an edge*). Yes, I'm sure.

The emotional moat he's built up is too wide to be crossed at this point. Linda kisses him lightly on the cheek, then rises and moves to the kitchen. She pauses at the door, looking back at him, a tentative smile on her face, but Gale's expression doesn't match or encourage the smile. Disheartened, Linda leaves the room.

Tight on Gale

His hand moves to the injured knee, the cast large beneath the trouser leg. Alone, the mask falters slightly and the fear is unmistakable. Then, after a moment or two, we, and Gale, start to hear the sound of a man singing. We've heard the song before. It's Brian singing the Wake Forest fight song. Gale looks with disbelief toward another door off of the living room. Using the canes, Gale pulls himself to an upright position and makes his way slowly across the room to the door. He pulls it open.

Angle down basement stairway

The singing is louder now. A beat, then Brian's smiling face appears at the bottom. He's wearing old clothes, carries a crescent wrench in one hand.

BRIAN. Hey, Magic . . . thought you'd never get here.

He moves back out of sight and we hear the sound of something metal being tapped upon. Gale enters frame and starts down the steps carefully.

GALE. Pic—what are you doing down there?

Interior—Basement—Full shot—Day

This is not a recreation room. The walls are cement block, gun-metal gray; a washer and dryer are in a corner. Opposite them, Brian Piccolo is tightening bolts on a metal framework that will eventually be used as a leg-lift machine. Gale negotiates the last few steps.

BRIAN. It's not a bad act, Gale, but Peg Leg Bates does it better.
GALE *(indicating machine)*. What's that supposed to be?
BRIAN. It's not "supposed" to be anything but what it is—a leg-lift machine.
GALE. What for?
BRIAN. What *for?* Gale—getting that knee back into shape is not going to be a take-it-easy number. If you're afraid, that's understandable, but . . .
GALE *(hard)*. I am *not* afraid!

Piccolo is out of patience. He picks up the tools and starts for the stairway.

BRIAN *(quietly)*. You ought to be, Gale.
GALE. Pic, maybe you think this is a real friendly thing you're doing, but . . .
BRIAN. And you can put that in your ditty bag, too, you stupid jackass—friendship hasn't got one thing to do with this. . . .

Piccolo is halfway up the steps now. He stops, looking back at Gale, weighing whether or not to go on. Sayers's expression is stubborn and angry, but no more so than Brian's. A beat, then Brian sits on one of the steps.

BRIAN. Gale—when I was in high school—I was one of the best backs in the state. Unfortunately for me, *the* best back in the state, Tucker Fredrickson, went to the same school. And the colleges would come down to watch us and Tuck ended up at Auburn—and I ended up at Wake Forest. Good school, nice place, but not exactly center ring, you follow?

(beat)

So—I work my butt off at Forest. And my senior year—I led the nation in rushing and scoring. ... *(Softly)* I mean—I led the *entire* nation.

(beat)

So, I look around for a pro team, and I pick the Bears. Then, who else comes to the Bears—Sayers. Big gun from a big school, and I'm number two all over again.

(beat)

Well, Gale—I'm number one guy now, but for all the wrong reasons. And if you don't come back one hundred percent, people are always going to say that I got in on a pass, a lucky break, and I won't take it that way. *(Rises)* I am going to beat you, Magic, but it won't mean a thing unless you're at your best, not one second slower, one degree weaker. I'm going to work your tail off getting you into shape again—for *my* sake.

Full shot

Brian turns and goes to the top of the stairs. Gale stands there, rage stilled, cooled, then turns, looking steadily at the leg-lift machine. He moves to it, running his fingertips over it lightly, seeking reassurance from the chilled metal.

Direct cut to:

Exterior—City park—Day—On Gale

It's a blustery, cold day. The wind drives ribbons of dry snow along the walk. Gale moves toward us, using a wooden cane, the limp noticeable but not as bad as previously seen. He wears an overcoat, the collar turned up, and a grim expression. In his free hand he carries a small radio. A sportscaster is heard over the sound of the wind.

ANNOUNCER *(voice-over)*. And in Los Angeles, the Chicago Bears trimmed the Rams by a score of seventeen to sixteen. Quarterback Jack Concannon was eight for fourteen passing, and the running game was ably manned by Brian Piccolo, who gained 105 yards in fourteen carries. Piccolo was awarded the game ball.

Gale is adjacent to a litter basket. He stops for a beat, his back to us, then deposits the cane into the basket. His step seems to have more drive to it when he moves on.

Direct cut to:

Exterior—Park area—Day—On Gale
It's early morning as Gale, dressed in a sweatsuit, comes jogging toward us. His expression is stoic, the pace quite slow, the sort of speed one recommends to those just discharged from the hospital after hernial surgery. But the pace is steady and dogged.

DR. FOX *(voice-over)*. *(Filter)* Hello?

BRIAN *(voice-over)*. *(Filter)* Dr. Fox? This is Brian Piccolo. How's he doing?

DR. FOX *(voice-over)*. *(Filter)* Very well, I think. Though it's boring going through those exercises all by yourself. It's drudgery and it's painful, and a lot of people just give up when they're alone in that situation.

Direct cut to:

Interior—Sayers's basement—Night—Tight on Gale
Gale is lying on his back, feet in the air, as he strains to lift the platform bearing a sizable portion of weights. He's drenched with sweat, puffing. We pan up from his face to the knee, seeing the wicked-looking scar that creases the flesh. As he starts to lift the platform, we pull back to reveal Piccolo seated nearby. He has a small kitchen egg timer in his hand.

BRIAN. And—ten. *(Setting timer)* Minute rest, then one more set.

GALE. *Another* one?

BRIAN. Last one tonight. Hang in there.

Gale remains on the floor under the weight machine. He sighs, getting his breath back.

BRIAN. How's the knee feel?

GALE *(dispirited)*. Oh, one day it feels as strong as ever; the next day it's like I got spaghetti for ligaments.

   (beat)

BRIAN. You know—if it doesn't come all the way back—it won't be the end of the world, Gale.

GALE. That so?

BRIAN. Football's terrific, man, but it's still just a job.

GALE. It's the only job I know how to do.

   (beat)

I'm not like you—I can't talk and all that stuff.

BRIAN. Talking now . . .

GALE. It's different.

   (beat)

BRIAN. You'll learn how to talk, once you find something that's got to be said.

The egg timer chirps once and Gale lifts his legs to the underside of the platform bearing the weights.

BRIAN. Third set. Ten reps. *Go.*

Gale starts to lift. The first three or four times go smoothly enough, but about halfway through the fifth one . . .

GALE *(straining)*. I'll never make ten, man—no juice left . . .

BRIAN. Don't bone me! Come on, Magic! Hang tough! Five. Way to go—six—lookin' good, Magic. Come on. . . .

GALE. No—way . . .

BRIAN. You aren't getting out that easy! Come on! You can

do it! Seven! Fantastic! Three more, man! Work on it! Are these the legs of a murderer? Come on, Gale! Eight! Got it! Two more!

GALE. No—way . . .

Tight on Brian

He is leaning over Gale, mind seeking a ploy.

BRIAN. Can't make it, huh, weakling? Giving up, is that it? Is that what you're doing?

Tight on Gale

Looking up at Brian expressionlessly—then a stifled laugh breaks from his lips. He smiles.

GALE. Come on, man—don't make me laugh.

Gale starts to laugh and lets the weights come to rest on the stops. Brian just stands there without any comprehension of how his maneuver could have backfired so badly.

Direct cut to:

Exterior wooded area—Day—Long shot

Brian and Gale move along a narrow dirt road that winds through the trees. Their pace is no longer that of a jog, but one more suited to a brisk 880.

Closer—Trucking

We move back in front of the two of them as they run, both in control, arms pumping smoothly, the motion fluid and easy. After a few seconds, Brian looks over briefly at Gale, then he picks up the pace a little, opening a few yards between them. Gale takes this with some surprise but matches Brian and closes the gap. But it's only temporary, for Brian ups the ante once more, the pace now at 440 clip. Gale's eyes flash as Brian moves away, but he picks it up again. He's shoulder to shoulder with Pic.

BRIAN. A beer for the first man to the bridge!
GALE. You're on!

Different angle
Brian peels off from the road and crashes into the trees flanking the road. Gale is a little surprised at this cross-country route, but he's right after Brian, though he's got about five or six yards to make up due to the momentary hesitation.

On Brian
There are no paths here, no easy routes. The trees and shrubs make it necessary to dart this way and that, hurdle logs, scramble up steep slopes and gullies. Brian is in the lead, but Gale's responding to the challenge, charging after him at full bore.

Various cuts—The chase
The two of them are bound together by an invisible rope, though the rope has developed a tendency to shrink slightly. It's almost imperceptible, but Gale is making up ground on Brian. They come to a creek bed five or six inches deep, and as they go splashing through it, we go to slow motion—droplets exploding into the sunlight, the two men calling on reserves from deep within. The small stream dwindles to loose shale.

The fall
A scant step behind Piccolo, Gale loses his footing on the stones and takes a head-over-heels tumble, a really bad one, pinwheeling over and over violently. Piccolo halts immediately, looking back at Gale with concern.

On Brian
He is gasping for breath, looking to Gale.

On Gale
He meets Brian's look. Every breath hurts, sears. He glances down at the knee, then stands slowly, brushing the stones from the palms of his hands. He meets Brian's look. He nods.

Full shot
Like catapults, they both turn and take off. They burst out of the trees, Gale a step behind. This is the final all-out sprint for the tape. Nothing held in reserve at this point, they pull great gulps of air in, straining, eyes frozen on the finish up ahead. And with each step, Gale moves up. An inch, no more, but that inch is repeated with each step, every stride bringing him closer to Brian's shoulder.

Long shot
As they near a small wooden footbridge, they move, it seems, as one, mirror images of black and white. They both literally hurl themselves at the imaginary tape and go tumbling across the bridge with their momentum, sprawling in the soft grass on the other side.

They are both lying there, having given it all they had to give. They're shiny as seals with perspiration, their eyes bright with fatigue, focusing on the blue sky overhead. After a long moment, they both sit up, shaky smiles on their faces, though they're still puffing like a Saint Bernard in Palm Springs.

BRIAN. I—think—I—owe—you—a—beer.
GALE *(shakes head)*. I—think—I—owe—you—a—lot—more—than—that.
BRIAN. Yeah—you're—healthy.
GALE. Yeah.

And they look at each other, the expressions of both growing a little serious, aware that, as friends, they are still competitors; there's only one brass ring on this merry-go-round.

Part Two

GIBRON *(voice-over)*. What do you think training camp is? You think training camp is some kind of picnic? Is that what you think? Because there's no man assured of a job around here, let me tell you, and if you think you are, then you got one more thing comin', gentlemen!

As Gibron's voice starts to come over, we also start to hear the sounds of the Chicago Bears calling out a cadence as they go through their calisthenics.

Hard cut to:

Exterior—Practice area—Day—Full shot
The backs step through the ropes, knees high. We pick up Gale going through the obstacle course, with Brian right behind him, both handling it with relative ease. We pan them, then all of them leave the frame to hold on the grizzled features of Coach Halas. His eyes are masked by dark glasses, but there's a smile tugging on the corners of his mouth.

Direct cut to:

Interior—Dormitory room—Night—On Gale
The playbook is in front of him. We pan across the room to find Brian, same look, same activity. A beat, then there is a knock on the door. Brian opens the door and reacts with some surprise on seeing Coach Halas standing in the hallway. He nods pleasantly. Gale, too, is surprised and sits up.

HALAS. Hello, Brian. Mind if I come in for a moment?
BRIAN. No, no. Of course not. Come on in, Coach.

And Halas comes in, moving by Brian. The two young men look to each other, neither having any notion that might explain this unprecedented visit.

HALAS. How's the knee, Gale?

GALE. Fine, Coach. Feels strong.

BRIAN. Look, if you want to talk to Gale, I can just walk on down to . . .

HALAS. No, actually, I'd like to talk to both of you.

Chilling portent. They both smile, as does Halas, but only the Old Man's has any relaxation in it. Long beat. Throat clearings from Gale and Brian.

BRIAN. Well—uh—how do things look this year, Coach?

HALAS. Fine. Just fine. Matter of fact, there's one boy I'm very impressed with. Brian, I wouldn't be surprised to see him replace you as number two halfback.

Halas lets the moment run on for a second.

HALAS. Because I'm making you number one fullback.

Tight on Brian
He sits there looking at Halas much as Papa Dionne must have looked at the doctor.

On Gale
Beaming, really and deeply pleased for his friend.

GALE. Hey, Pic—you and me the starting backfield—what do you say?

Full shot
Brian just shakes his head back and forth, an empty smile flopping about on his face.

GALE. Coach—I didn't think it was possible—but I think you finally found a way to shut him up!

Hard cut to:
NFL footage—Alternating between runs of Piccolo and Sayers

GALE (*voice-over*). Hey, Pic?

BRIAN (*voice-over*). Yeah?

GALE (*voice-over*). You know you got a four point three rushing average?

BRIAN (*voice-over*). No, man, but hum a few bars and I'll see if I can fake it.

GALE (*voice-over; overlapping*). Aw, *Pic* . . .

Exterior—Angle to football field—End zone

Brian breaks through a hole in the center of the line, keeping his feet as he gets to the end zone, flipping the ball high into the air. The first person to him is Gale, slapping him exuberantly on the back as they move with their teammates toward the bench.

Direct cut to:

Interior—Locker room—Day—Full shot

The team is being weighed in, Gibron by the scales, sliding the weights up and down the bar and calling out the result for each man. There is some good-natured catcalling as some of the larger linemen are weighed in and most of it is coming from Brian, who is next in line, with Gale close behind him. Brian takes his place. Gibron starts to readjust the weights.

BRIAN. Scrimmage tomorrow, Abe. Going to give us any trick plays?

GIBRON. Only trick I'd like to give you is how to keep some meat on you. You're down another pound.

BRIAN. But what's there is choice; admit it.

GIBRON. Two-o-six and a quarter. Skinniest fullback in the league.

BRIAN. Gibron, you run the fat off us, then complain that we're too thin. You're a hard man to please.

Brian grins, used to Gibron's grumbles, and moves off. Gale is next in line.

GIBRON. Ought to tell your Italian friend to load up on the pasta.

GALE. Probably just wants to be quicker, Gibron.

GIBRON. Well, it ain't workin'. He lost ten pounds and he's half a second slower over a forty-yard sprint. Lighter *and* slower don't total out to much of a threat, you know. (*Checks the weight*) One ninety-nine. Next.

We move with Gale as he steps off the scale, camera closing on him. He glances off at Gibron, then in the direction taken by Brian. His eyes are puzzled; it's a weird combination Gibron has pointed out. Strange. Unsettling. Gale lets it sink in.

Direct cut to:

NFL footage of Gale and Brian

Running the ball, alternating. Two cuts, the first being the best footage of Piccolo as either runner or receiver, the last being a punt return by Sayers that goes all the way. This final cut, the punt return, is to lead directly into the following staged sequence.

Angle to Bears' sideline

Gale comes off the field with the rest of the punt-return unit, among whom is Brian. Typically, Gale barely smiles at the congratulations he gets. He moves to the bench and sits, Brian by his side. They pull off their helmets, eyes on the game.

Closer angle—Gale and Brian

Both winded, but with one difference. Gale is clearly buoyed up, exhilarated. Brian simply seems tired.

GALE. Nice block.

BRIAN. Thanks.

(*beat*)

Must be ninety million pounds of pollen in the air.

Gale glances over at Brian casually and might see what we are now noting. Gale's respiration is swiftly slowing down, approaching normal. Brian's is not, he's still winded and badly so. Brian rises, moving for the water bucket near the phone desk. Gale watches him, then rises, moving for the sidelines to view the upcoming kickoff, camera moving with him. He finds an opening among the men standing there; then, in the hush just prior to the kicker's runup, the sound of Brian coughing. Gale turns back.

His point of view—On Brian
The roar of the crowd overwhelms the sound of Piccolo's coughing. He takes down a fair amount of water, but that doesn't help. Brian coughs once more, though it's more evident in the motion of his shoulders and chest than in a sound; he's making an effort to stifle the cough.

GALE. You ought to get Fox to give you something for that hay fever.

BRIAN. He did. Doesn't help. The only thing I'm allergic to is Ray Nitschke. *(Yelling)* All right, Butkus! Stick it in their ear, babe!

Brian moves off, back toward the bench. Gale looks to the playing field, but his thoughts are elsewhere. He glances back.

His point of view—Angle to Piccolo
Seated once more on the bench, his helmet off, still using more effort than one would expect to get his wind back. He sees Gale looking at him and smiles, giving a "thumbs-up" sign.

On Gale
Nodding, returning both the smile and the sign, and both are, at one and the same time, lies and prayers.

Direct cut to:
Interior—Bears' locker room—Day—Full shot
Most of the players are dressed now, or seated in front of their lockers tying their shoes. We find Halas as he comes out of his

office, his expression somber. He pulls up a stool beside Gale and sits, drained, enervated.

GALE. Lookin' at you, I'd never know we won the game.
HALAS *(small smile)*. I don't feel very much like a winner at the moment.
GALE. Why not?

A deep breath, a gathering of his forces.

HALAS. Gale, I'm sending Brian Piccolo back to Chicago. He won't make the rest of the road trip with us. Ralph Kurek's going to start next week.
   (beat)
GALE. Why?
HALAS. Because I've had a policy on this team from the very start—the best player plays, no exceptions. And right now—Kurek is the best player.
GALE. Look, a lot of guys take a while to get on track for a season, slow starters, and . . .
HALAS *(finishing for him)*. And Brian Piccolo has never been one of those guys, Gale. He's always been in shape, able to give one hundred percent. But he isn't doing that anymore, and that worries me. *(With regret)* I don't know why—something physical—or whether he's got personal problems, something with his wife or children—but the truth is that something is taking the edge off of him—and I want to find out what that something is. For his sake and the team's. Can't afford to lose a back that good.
GALE *(resigned)*. When's he going to find out?
HALAS. Abe's telling him now. That's why I didn't want you to go right back to the hotel.
GALE. Wouldn't want to be in Abe's shoes about now. . . .
HALAS. I wouldn't want to be in *your* shoes about ten minutes from now.

Direct cut to:
Interior—Hotel room—Night—On suitcase
A bundle of wadded-up clothes is thrown into the suitcase. We pull back to reveal Piccolo in the act of packing, moving from closet and dresser to the suitcase on the bed. Gale maintains a low profile, not wanting to draw any fire from Brian.

BRIAN. Who'd believe it? I mean, really, who'd believe it!

GALE. Halas just wants you to see the doctor, and . . .

BRIAN. Halas doesn't know what he wants! Gibron's his boy and you should have heard *that* lecture! Kept telling me to patch things up with Joy. I tell him things are fine with me and Joy. And he just smiles that Father Flanagan smile of his and says I shouldn't be afraid to level with him.

GALE. Pic, be fair, now. Dr. Fox says that . . .

BRIAN. Oh, spare me any crud about our great team doctor. Wants me to get a physical for the cough, right? No allergy. Then what is it, I say! Want to hear what he says? *Could* be a virus. *Could* be a staph infection. *Could* be any one of a thousand things. It's like being treated in a Chinese restaurant—two from column A, three from column B!

GALE. He's just trying to help, Pic. . . .

A beat, then Brian sits on the bed, calming somewhat, but still angry and frustrated.

BRIAN. Yeah—I suppose you're right—but it's all so pointless, Gale. I know perfectly well what's wrong with me.

He looks over at Gale, eyes radiating sincerity.

BRIAN. Gale—I think I'm pregnant.

Direct cut to:
Interior—Visiting team locker room—Day—Full shot

The Chicago Bears suit up. Linemen pound each other's shoulder pads to a tighter fit. Some of the players sit in front of their lockers, wide-eyed, seeing nothing. Others move about nervously, bouncing on the balls of their feet, trembling with caged energy.

Angle to training table
Gale is having his ankle wrapped tightly with adhesive tape. His face has the look of a carving—somber, dark, guarded. The trainer finishes the job and Gale nods his thanks, moving off the table, another man following behind him at once. We move with him as he strides toward a door at the other end of the locker room. He passes by Gibron, who is going over the attack plan with Concannon and the second-string quarterback, past linemen who are simply yelling at each other, wordless growls and bellows. Gale stops in front of the door bearing the word COACH. *He knocks on the door.*

HALAS *(offstage).* Come in.

Interior—The coach's office—Day—Full shot
Halas is seated behind the desk, hat and dark glasses on. Ed McCaskey is at a water cooler in the corner, drawing a paper cup out of the container, using the water to wash down a pill. At first, both men seem quite normal, but it's a facade and one that's being eroded with each passing second.

GALE. Which end of the field you want me to take if we lose the toss?

McCaskey and Halas stare at him for a second, then look to each other. Gale is a little baffled by the delay; the question is a standard one. Some kind of communication is going on between the two older men. They nod.

HALAS. Come on in, Gale. Close the door.

There is something in that tone, something vulnerable and sad, out of key. Gale steps into the room and closes the door as requested. There is a short silence, each of the other men hoping they'll not have to take the lead.

HALAS. Gale—we've just had a phone call from Memorial Hospital. . . .

Halas removes the glasses. His eyes are red. He takes a breath.

HALAS. Brian Piccolo has cancer.

Awe has within it an element of fear, of facing something so basic, so large, that one cannot ever truly cope with it. Gale reacts with prayerful disbelief and awe.

GALE. Oh, God . . .

Full shot
Halas kneads the bridge of his nose, the eyes closed as if hoping the curtain of his eyelids will allow time for a scene change.

HALAS. They've scheduled an operation for tomorrow morning.
GALE *(feeling).* An operation to do what?
MCCASKEY *(evenly, calmly).* Gale, they've got to remove part of Brian's right lung.

This strikes Gale like a whiplash. He starts to sink weakly into a nearby chair, and as he does so the frame freezes several times, giving the same look associated with the knee injury. As he sinks into the chair, the image moves with stuttering, uneven speed.

HALAS *(offstage).* The doctors don't have any explanation, Gale. It must be something Brian has carried around inside him all his life. What set it off, they don't know. As to whether or not they found it in time—well, they don't know that either, I'm afraid.

Gale's eyes are glazed. His spirit has been blindsided. Halas and McCaskey are no less affected.

MCCASKEY *(to Halas)*. Who tells them?

Halas sighs, nodding.

HALAS. I know. It's my responsibility and I'll . . .
GALE *(interrupting)*. I'll tell them.
HALAS *(surprised)*. You, Gale?
GALE *(rising)*. That's right, me. I'll tell them. Let's go. *(To McCaskey)* Does Linda know?
MCCASKEY. I don't think so. . . .
GALE. Call her and tell her.

He pulls open the door, looking to Halas. The Coach and McCaskey trade a swift look, then Halas gets to his feet. As he moves to the door, McCaskey picks up the phone on the desk and starts to dial.

Interior—The locker room—Day—Full shot
Halas and Gale come out of the Coach's room. Halas's presence is noted quickly and the players gather around in a loose semi-circle. Gale appears very much in control of himself, in command of the situation.

HALAS *(to players)*. Gale has got something he'd like to say to you all. Gale . . .

Gale attempts to sustain eye contact with the other members of the team, but it swiftly becomes clear to him that he can't make it. Initially, his voice is strong and clear, but he can't hold it there for long.

GALE. You—you all know that we hand out a game ball to the outstanding player. Well, I'd like to change that a little. We just got word that Brian Piccolo—that he's sick. Very sick. It looks like—uh—that he might not ever play football again—or—for a long time. . . .

(beat)

And—I think we should all dedicate ourselves to—give our maximum effort to win this ball game and give the game ball to Pic. We can all sign it and take it up to him at the hosp . . .

His voice tightens with abrupt anguish. He turns away, hiding his tears.

GALE *(continuing, softly)*. Oh, my *God* . . .

Fade Out.
Fade In:
Interior—Brian's hospital room—Day—Tight on Brian
Garbed in hospital gown, looking strangely out of place, a young man of two hundred pounds is in something approximating a doll's wardrobe. He's grinning from ear to ear, holding up the front page of the sports section, the headline of which reads COLTS DUMP BEARS 24–21.

BRIAN *(voice-over)*. Fantastic! Who'd believe it! Sayers, you've got great moves on the field, but in the locker room, I've got to tell you, you're a klutz! When you dedicate a game to someone, you are then supposed to go out and *win* the game, idiot! Pat O'Brien never said, "Blow one for the Gipper," you know.

Full shot
Gale and Jack Concannon stand at the end of the bed. At a small table near the window, the flowers and cards have been cleared away by J. C. Caroline and a few other players. In place of these niceties, they are opening up two cartons of pizza and two six-packs of beer. Joy Piccolo stands next to her husband.

GALE. Bad—you are so bad.
CAROLINE. We probably would have won if Concannon had called that trap play more, but he hates to use it unless you're there for the repeat.

The men at the table have started putting pieces of pizza on paper napkins and begin to distribute them.

JOY. Brian, do you think this is such a good idea? I mean, pepperoni pizza and beer *isn't* on your diet.

BRIAN. Joy—are you telling me as I lie on this bed of pain, my body whittled away at by a ruthless band of strangers with Exacto knives—are you telling me I can't have any *pizza?*

Joy studies Brian, then looks to the other men. She shakes her head, exasperated and loving them all very much.

JOY. Pass the pizza, please. . . .

With smiles, the others crowd around the bed as Joy moves to the table. After a second or two to get the first bite down:

BRIAN. Hey—who wants to see my scar?

Instant negative replies from them all. As these trail off, the door is opened offstage and they all look around. A nurse enters. She gazes at her patient, who has just had a lung removed, as he visits with his wife and friends, all of whom have pizza in hand.

NURSE. *Out! Now! No* discussion! *Out!*

Full shot
Gale, Butkus, Concannon, Caroline, and Mayes quickly gather up the pizza cartons and head for the door, ad-libbing farewells, ducking their heads like schoolboys as they pass by the nurse. Gale is the last in line. Joy straightens up from kissing Brian goodbye.

BRIAN. Hey, take Gale down and have him give that little girl his autograph, will you? *(To Gale)* Little girl I met the day I came in here. We had our operations on the same day. Told her I'd get your autograph. You don't mind, do you?

GALE. No problem. Be glad to.

JOY. I'll see you tonight.

He blows a kiss at her and they all leave. The nurse holds for a second in the door, reinforcing her disapproval of Brian's ways. She sighs and steps out of the door. Once it's closed, Brian throws back the covers and puts his feet over the side. There's a good deal of strain and discomfort involved, but it's well within Brian's tolerance. He stands with his back to the window, then starts for the door, his gait a shuffle.

BRIAN. There he goes, sports fans—can you believe it— power, speed, grace, and agility all wrapped up in . . .

Brian halts as the door is opened once again by the nurse. Their eyes fight to a draw.

BRIAN. Don't come any closer, Miss Furman. White lisle stockings turn me on!

Direct cut to:

Children's ward—Angle to nurses' station

The walls here are festooned with crayon drawings made by the patients. The nurses' station has a number of stuffed animals on the counter. As Joy and Gale approach, one of the nurses hangs up the phone and turns to them with a pleasant smile.

NURSE #2. May I help you?

JOY. My name's Mrs. Piccolo. My husband's a patient on the third floor and he told me about a little girl—Patti Lucas—who wanted this gentleman's autograph.

The nurse nods nicely, holding up a finger as she flips swiftly through the Rolodex in front of her.

NURSE #2. I'm sorry, Mrs. Piccolo—Patti isn't with us any- more.

JOY. Well, do you have a home address? My husband wanted her to have the autograph very much.

(beat)

NURSE #2. Mrs. Piccolo—Patti's dead. She passed away early this morning.

Gale places his hand gently on Joy's shoulder. Joy nods, forcing a smile mouthing the "thank you," though her voice is absent. Gale is a few feet behind her as they start back for the elevator bank.

Direct cut to:

NFL footage of Gale in an end run, preferably slow motion

The crowd noise is at a frenzied peak; then the frame freezes.

BRIAN *(voice-over).* Look at that knee, will you? That thing is really beautiful!

Exterior—Hospital grounds—Day—Full shot
Brian is wheeled out onto the hospital lawn. He's looking at a sports magazine, which he holds up so Joy can see the picture. They stop beneath a large tree bordering the walk.

BRIAN. Nothing wrong with that knee; I'll tell you that.
JOY. Congratulations, Dr. Piccolo.
BRIAN. Yeah—but you know what—I've been thinking. With Gale healthy, and Ralph Kurek healthy—I'm going to have a rough time getting back into the lineup next year. And I was thinking—what's so difficult about being a kicker? I mean, I wonder if it's something you can teach yourself. 'Cause you don't need a lot of wind or stamina or size . . .

He looks down at Joy and the look on her face is weakening, hopeful still, but with more effort required on her part with each day that goes by. Brian reads that look like a compass.

BRIAN. All right, Gloomy Gus—what do you think of my brainstorm?

JOY *(floundering)*. Well—I don't know, Brian—I'm no expert on kickers and things . . .

BRIAN. You just did an end run that Red Grange would be proud to call his own.

JOY. Don't make fun of me, Brian. I'm scared.

BRIAN *(evenly)*. What of?

JOY *(sputtering with disbelief)*. What *of* ? What *of* ? You can't be serious! You know perfectly well what of!

BRIAN *(absolutely sincere)*. No, I don't, Joy. I swear to God I don't. *(Taking her hands)* Look—I'm no idiot.—This thing is bad—I know that—but it's a detour, Joy—that's all. It's not going to stop me because I'm not going to *let* it stop me. No way . . . *(Quietly)* I've got too much to do yet, Joy.

Her face in his hands, Brian bends to kiss Joy. As their lips meet, we start to boom up and back. Joy leans her head against Brian's knee, his hand stroking her hair.

Direct cut to:

NFL footage of Sayers
Fielding a punt, signaling for a fair catch, then deciding to let it roll. And roll it does, further and further back toward his own goal. By the time he realizes he should have caught it, there are a number of defensive men all around the ball, making any return impossible. From the time the ball struck earth and took off, we have heard:

BRIAN *(voice-over)*. Pick it up! Pick it up, dummy! Gale! Joy, look at him!

NURSE *(voice-over)*. Now, Mr. Piccolo, calm down.

BRIAN *(voice-over)*. Calm down? How can I calm down? You'd think the ball was wearing a white sheet.

Direct cut to:

Interior—Hotel room—Night—Full shot
Gale is on the bed, shoes off, talking on the phone with Brian, the mood one of good-natured give-and-take. Seated on the

other bed is a football player, Gale's new roommate. There is a room-service cart in evidence, remnants there of sandwiches and glasses of milk. We intercut this with Brian in his hospital room. There is no one else present with Brian.

GALE. Well, I was going to catch it, but when it started coming down, I said I wonder what Pic would do in a situation like this, and ducking seemed to be the answer.

BRIAN. Well, at least you won the game.

GALE. That's right.

BRIAN. Didn't dedicate this one to me, though, did you?

In the hotel room, there is a knock on the door. The other player goes to answer it. He opens the door to reveal a hotel official, who exchanges a few words with the football player, then is allowed into the room.

GALE. Nope. Dedicated this one to Butkus.

BRIAN. Why?

GALE. He threatened us.

   (beat)

How you doin'? Pic? Really?

BRIAN. Hanging in there, Magic. Doing what they tell me to do. You could do me a favor, though.

GALE. You got it. Name it.

BRIAN. Call Joy, will you? When she left tonight, she was really down. I never saw her that down.

GALE. I'll call her as soon as I get back.

BRIAN. Thanks, I appreciate it.

GALE. Okay. Goodnight.

BRIAN. Goodnight.

Gale hangs up, then looks a question to the hotel clerk.

HOTEL OFFICIAL. Mr. Sayers, while you were on the phone, there was a lady who called. She seemed very upset.

He hands Gale a piece of folded paper. Gale unfolds it.

HOTEL OFFICIAL. I hope I've not overstepped my authority.
PLAYER. I'm sure you did the right thing. Thank you very much.

He ushers the hotel official out the door, closes it, then glances back at Gale, who sags, drained.

GALE. It's Joy Piccolo. She says it's urgent.

Direct cut to:
Interior—Piccolo living room—Night—On clock
The time is 3:30. We pull back to reveal Joy, in robe and slippers, pouring coffee for Gale and Linda. The Sayerses have dumped their coats on the couch.

JOY. I know it's an awful thing, to make you fly all the way back here in the middle of the night, but . . .
GALE. It doesn't bother me, so don't let it bother you.

Joy smiles feebly and sits, her hands tightly intertwined, struggling to maintain her composure. A long beat.

LINDA. Just say it, Joy. . . .

Joy nods, a childlike move.

JOY. They found more of the tumor. . . .

The tears come. Her face twists, crumpling under the terror and the fear. Linda moves to her, holding her, both women rocking back and forth. Gale swallows bitterly, probably wishing he was strong enough to cry. He pulls a handkerchief out of his pocket and places it on the coffee table within Joy's reach. She nods her appreciation, dabbing at her eyes.

JOY. They told me today—they want to operate again—and I was going to tell Brian—but—I couldn't, Gale. I don't know whether or not he can take the disappointment. And if he can't—I know *I* can't.
    (beat)

The doctor is going to tell him tomorrow morning. If you could be there when he finds out—it might help.

GALE. I'll be there, Joy.

Direct cut to:

Interior—Brian's room—Day—On football game

This is a "board game" with charts and dice and miniature scoreboard. As we pull back, we find Brian and Gale seated on opposite sides of the small table near the window. They both roll their dice.

GALE. What'd you try?

BRIAN. End run.

GALE. Oh, Lordy—I was in a blitz.

Brian starts to consult the complicated chart that will give him the results of the play.

GALE *(indicating game chart).* Well—did you gain or what?

The door is opened by Mr. Eberle, a nervous, uncertain sort, more at home with facts and figures than flesh and blood. A name tag hangs from the lapel of his lab coat. Brian looks up with a smile.

BRIAN. Hi. Can I help you?

EBERLE. Well, I'm sorry if I'm disturbing anything . . .

BRIAN. Don't worry—I can beat him later. What can I do for you?

EBERLE *(rummaging through papers).* I know this is a bother at a time like this, Mr. Piccolo, but hospitals have their rules and regulations, you see, and I'll need your signature on this surgical consent for the operation.

He hands Brian the piece of paper, but Brian is scarcely aware of it. He looks at Eberle uncomprehendingly, stunned. Gale is searching for a way to ease this, but before he can locate his voice, Eberle notes the bewilderment on Brian's face.

EBERLE. The doctor *has* been here, hasn't he? He's talked with you, I mean?

BRIAN. No . . .

EBERLE *(looking to watch)*. Oh—well, I suppose I might be running a little ahead of my schedule today. Perhaps I better come back after the doctor has . . .

BRIAN. What would the doctor have to say to me? Man, I've *had* my operation, *right*?

Silence, and that's the worst answer there can be. Eberle can't meet Brian's look. After a beat, Brian looks over slowly to Gale.

BRIAN. Talk to me, Magic. . . .

Gale discovers his voice after a second, but it emerges with anguish.

GALE. The tests show—there's more of the tumor than they thought, Pic. They have to operate again. . . .

Once more, Eberle, seeking nothing more than escape, steps forward, holding out the surgical consent and a fountain pen.

EBERLE. So, if you'll just sign the consent, Mr. . . .

BRIAN *(turning away)*. No!

EBERLE. But putting this off won't be . . .

BRIAN. Are you deaf? I said *no!*

EBERLE. Mr. Sayers—can't you talk to your friend?

Brian has moved to the window, shoulders hunched as if gathering himself for a blow of enormous force. Gale looks at him, then turns to Eberle.

GALE. No, Mr. Eberle, I think I'd rather talk to *you*.

EBERLE. But . . .

GALE. Brian is a professional athlete, Mr. Eberle. And a professional gets into a habit after a while. He gets himself ready for a game mentally as well as physically. Because he knows those two things are all tied up together. And there's a clock going inside him, so that when the game starts, he's one hundred percent mentally and physically. And what Pic is saying to you now is that you're scheduling this game before he can get ready. Couldn't it wait until over the weekend?

EBERLE. Well, yes, it *could,* but . . .

GALE. Then *let* it.

EBERLE *(a beat, looks to Brian).* First thing Monday morning, Mr. Piccolo.

BRIAN. Okay.

EBERLE. I'll see you then.

Gale looks back to Brian, who continues to gaze out the window. A beat, as Brian strains to salvage some control.

BRIAN. Thanks, Gale . . .

GALE. No sweat.

BRIAN. Thought you were the guy who didn't talk very well.

GALE. Well—I roomed with an Italian; you know how they are.

Brian turns away from the window. He moves back to the game board, idly scanning the setup. A beat, then a small smile appears on his face.

BRIAN. Guess what? I scored a touchdown.

We hold on Brian.

                                            Cut to black over following:

NURSE #1'S VOICE. Good morning, Mr. Piccolo. Time to wake up now.

                                                          Fade In:

Medium shot—Nurse #1

She is looking into lens, smiling Cheshirely, a hypodermic needle in hand.

NURSE #1. I'm going to give you a little shot to help you relax, Mr. Piccolo. You'll be going up to the operating room in about an hour.

BRIAN (*offstage*). My wife here?

NURSE #1. You'll see her when you come down, Mr. Piccolo. Now, this won't hurt a bit.

BRIAN (*offstage*). Yes—you're being very brave about it all.

Direct cut to:

Interior—Operating room—Up angle

A doctor, masked and gowned, leans into the lens, arms held up away from his body.

DOCTOR. Mr. Piccolo—we're going to put you to sleep now. . . .

BRIAN (offstage). That's the—worst—choice of words—I ever heard in my life. . . .

As we start a slow fade to black, we begin to hear the sound of applause, growing louder and louder with each second. Then, in utter darkness:

M.C. (*offstage*). Gale Sayers!!!

Cut to:

Interior—Banquet hall—Night—Tight on Gale

Dressed in a tuxedo, Gale starts as he becomes aware of the explosion of sounds being directed at him. Other men at his table poke Gale, all laughing as they urge him to his feet. Startled, he rises and the camera pans him as he is almost passed along from table to table.

The dais

Gale smiles, still at a loss, and moves toward the toastmaster, who is holding out a large trophy to him. As Gale accepts the trophy with a muttered thank you the applause builds once more. Gale looks down at the inscription on the trophy.

Insert—The inscription
*It reads "George S. Halas Award—Most Courageous Player—
to Gale Sayers."*

Tight on Gale
*He looks out, nodding acknowledgment to the applause. Slowly
it starts to trail off, then dies. A moment of throat clearings,
chairs shifting into better positions. When it is absolutely still,
Gale begins to speak.*

GALE. I'd like to say a few words about a guy I know—a
friend of mine. His name is Brian Piccolo and he has the
heart of a giant—and that rare form of courage that
allows him to kid himself and his opponent—cancer. He
has the mental attitude that makes me proud to have a
friend who spells out courage twenty-four hours a day,
every day of his life.

Gale takes a sip of water.

GALE. You flatter me by giving me this award—but I tell
you here and now I accept it for Brian Piccolo. Brian
Piccolo is the man of courage who should receive the
George S. Halas Award. It is mine tonight; it is Brian
Piccolo's tomorrow.

*Not a sound out there. Gale clutches the award tightly and his
eyes sparkle with tears. No attempt is made to hide those
tears.*

GALE. I love Brian Piccolo—and I'd like all of you to love
him, too. And, tonight—when you hit your knees . . .
   (beat)
Please ask God to love him. . . .

*Gale steps quickly out of the spotlight. We hold on the empty
circle for several seconds before the sound comes. First, one or
two people, then more, and swiftly an avalanche of thunder.*

Direct cut to:
Interior—Brian's hospital room—Day—On Brian
Joy places the phone on the pillow next to him. When the angle widens, we see Linda is also present. There is an IV stand next to the bed, a tank of oxygen in the corner. Brian's face is drawn, the flesh pallid and shiny. We intercut the conversation with Gale in his hotel room.

BRIAN. Hi, Magic . . .
GALE. How are you, Pic?
BRIAN. Oh, hangin' in there . . .
  (beat)
Heard what you did at the banquet. If you were here, I'd kiss you. . . .
GALE. Glad I'm not there, then.
BRIAN. Hey, Gale? They said you gave me a pint of blood. Is that true?
GALE. Yeah.
BRIAN. That explains it, then.
GALE. Explains what?
BRIAN. I've had this craving for chitlins all day.

Gale smiles on the other end.

GALE. I'll be in tomorrow morning, man. I'll see you then.
BRIAN. Yeah—I ain't going nowhere. . . .

Joy takes the phone and hands it to Linda, who takes the receiver to the window where the cradle is located. Camera closes on Linda, who raises the phone to her ear.

LINDA. Gale?
GALE. How is he, Linda? *Really?*
LINDA *(softly, yet urgently)*. Hurry. Gale—please hurry.

Direct cut to:
Interior—Brian's room—On Ed McCaskey
He is seated in a chair by the door, a continuous caressing of

rosary beads sliding through his fingers. The room is striped with sunlight from the partially closed Venetian blinds. The door is opened and Gale and Linda come in. Brian's eyes are closed, and his frame seems small beneath the blankets. Joy bends to him as Gale moves quietly to the other side of the bed, Linda holding by the door.

JOY. Brian—Gale's here.

Closer angle—Gale and Brian
Brian's hand comes up from the sheet in greeting. Gale takes the hand in his. Brian's words come slowly, breath on a ration.

BRIAN. Hello, Magic.
GALE *(after a beat)*. How's it going, Pic?
BRIAN. It's fourth and eight, man—but they won't let me punt.
GALE. Go for it, then.
BRIAN. I'm trying, Gale—God, how I'm trying. . . .

Suddenly Brian's head snaps back, his hand convulsing on Gale's. Tears spilling down her cheeks, Joy leans close to her husband.
   Seconds go by. Then, slowly, Brian's body relaxes and his head touches the pillow. Joy blots the perspiration from his brow. His eye goes to Gale.

BRIAN. Remember that first year . . . couldn't get a word out of you . . .
GALE. Couldn't get you to shut up . . .
BRIAN. Remember how you got me with those mashed potatoes . . .
GALE. You deserved it—the way you sang that dumb fight song—twice, you did it—at camp, and that time down in my basement . . .
   (beat)
And that 32 trap play—remember that?

BRIAN. Yeah. How could I forget?

There is a pause. Brian's look turns reflective. He smiles.

BRIAN. You taught me a lot about running, Gale. I appreciate it.

GALE. I wouldn't be running if I hadn't had you pushin' me—helping me . . .

BRIAN. I'll get you next training camp. . . .

GALE. I'll be waiting. . . .

BRIAN. Yeah . . . *(A sigh)* Gale, I'm feeling kind of punk. . . . I think I'll sack out for a while, okay?

GALE. Sure thing.

Angle to their hands
Gale gently lets go of Brian's hand, which falls limply back onto the sheet. Gale's hand rests on the other for a beat, then he moves away.

Full shot
The nurse opens the door for Gale and Linda. He stops, looking back, his voice choked.

GALE. See you tomorrow, Pic. . . .

Tight on Brian
He turns his head toward Gale, brings his gaze into focus. He lifts the hand closest to the door and gives a "thumbs-up."

BRIAN. If you say so. . . .

Offstage, the sound of the door closing. Brian pulls Joy close to him, his arms about her. His eyes close, his breathing slackens. Joy's lips are close to Brian's ear.

JOY. I love you, Brian—I love you. . . .

Brian forces his eyes open and looks at her for a long beat. He finds one final smile.

BRIAN. Who'd believe it, Joy—who'd ever believe it. . . .

And Brian and Joy are close for the last time. This stillness will endure.

Dissolve to:

Exterior—Hospital parking lot—Night—On Gale and Linda
Arm in arm they move slowly along the line of cars in the parking lot until they come to their own. Gale opens the door on Linda's side and helps her in. As he closes the door, he looks to the hospital.

His point of view—Hospital window
Zooming in on McCaskey in Brian's room. He slowly closes the blinds.

Tight on Gale
He gazes at the hospital.

NARRATOR *(voice-over).* Brian Piccolo died of cancer at the age of twenty-six. He left a wife and three daughters.

Superimpose over the close shot of Gale Sayers in the parking lot, footage from the footrace between Gale and Brian, ending with slow motion of their contest that freezes on a tight shot of Brian.

NARRATOR *(voice-over).* He also left a great many loving friends who miss him and think of him often. But, when they think of him, it's not how he died that they remember but, rather, how he *lived*. . . .

   (beat)
How he *did* live . . .

And as Gale moves around to his side of the car and starts to get in, the image of Brian takes precedence, smiling and full of life. A good face to study for a moment or two.

Fade Out.

William Blinn
(1937–   )

William Blinn was born in Toledo, Ohio, and graduated from the American Academy of Dramatic Arts in New York City. He has written and produced teleplays for *The Wonder Years* and *Our House,* two syndicated television series about families. For his teleplay of *Brian's Song,* written for ABC's *Movie of the Week,* he received an Emmy, the George Foster Peabody Award, the Writer's Guild of America Award, and the Black Sports Magazine Award. *Brian's Song* also received a Congressional Record Commendation as "one of the truly moving television and screen achievements."